CUSTOMARY LAW OF AUSTRIC–SPEAKING TRIBES

CUSTOMARY LAW OF AUSTRIC-SPEAKING TRIBES

P.K. Bhowmick

PUBLICATIONS

KALPAZ PUBLICATIONS

DELHI - 110052

CUSTOMARY LAW OF AUSTRIC–SPEAKING TRIBES

(Anthropology)

Rs. 540/-

ISBN : 81-7835-099-8

Published in 2002 in India by
Kalpaz Publications
C-30, Satyawati Nagar
Ashok Vihar-III,
Delhi-110 052
e-mail : kalpaz@hotmail.com

Laser Typesetting: Grow Computers, Delhi
Printed at: Chawla Offset Press, New Delhi

Dedication

The book is dedicated in memory of my mother

CONTENTS

PREFACE

Tribal communities in the global context have different attributes and they vary from place to place as regards the nature of interactions. Indian situation varies as these communities are scheduled to have constitutional benefits. After independence many welfare programmes have been sponsored by the government and many more voluntary organisations have been involved for the advancement of the so-called down-trodden communities. Naturally, changes of some sort or other are noticed.

The communities have their own customs; sometimes they seem to turn backward with superstitions. In exceptional cases societies take revenge on them for breach of customs. According to Henry Maine (1946); 'except custom there is no written law in the world', and it is an accepted truth that custom may be either good or evil. Malinowski (1940) observes that 'all custom is law to the savage and that he has no law but his custom'. It is also an accepted fact that custom is a traditional or indigenous system of social control. Many customs prevalent in tribal societies are not yet known to others. This is because no proper study of these customs has as yet been made. But we feel that the sentimental values attached to certain customs should not generally be ignored, though these values vary from one society to another. However, as society does not remain static, many more changes are expected to take place. Under the present circumstances, due to spread of education or economic solvency, certain changes are definitely perceptible in tribal societies. This is likely to enable the tribal communities to develop a spirit of legal awareness. This will also help them to better the mode of tribal administration. Besides, knowledge of the customary laws of the tribals will reduce the possibilities of litigation. Anyway, a systematic investigation has been attempted in this monograph to explain the significance of customary laws in six Austric-speaking tribal groups of frontier Bengal.

I am thankful to the Ministry of Tribal Affairs for sanctioning my research proposal to examine the tribal conditions against the background of the customary law of Tribal communities. I am thankful to Sri P.K. Mohanty, IAS, the then Secretary to the Department, and his colleagues, Dr. P.K. Mohanty, Joint Director, and Sri R.C. Mahapatra, Research Officer, Ministry of Tribal Affairs, Government of India for their constant encouragement and support for this research work.

My Research Fellows, Dr. S.K. Kolay and Sri Ranjan Shasmal, deserve special credit as they had to work in difficult areas. Special thanks are due to Sri P.K. Bandyopadhyay, Hon'ble Judge at Bolpur court for his endeavour to steer clear of some problems which I faced, while analysing the data regarding customary law.

I am thankful to my friend, Professor P.K. Deb, who has gone through the typescript.

Lastly, I must thank Mr. Swapan Basu, Kalyani, for his prompt and careful typing of the manuscript.

I hope this report entitled *Customary Law of Austric-Speaking Tribes* will help the administration to understand the tribal problems and to overcome ambiguities, on the one hand, and to realise, on the other, how democracy has slowly slackened the tribal conservatism on account of spread of education, urbanisation and employment facilities at new interactional situations. More interactions have also indirectly helped some satellite groups to follow the customs of the stronger groups.

I am also thankful to Sri B.P. Garg of Kalpaz Publications, Delhi for undertaking this publication.

727, Lake Town
Kolkata-700089

P.K. Bhowmick

March, 2002

Chapter One

INTRODUCTION

I

Men, in all times and climes, have to adjust themselves with varied situations - they may be in isolated hill tops, amidst merciless deserts, or may be in the lateritic undulations, clothed with patchy or deep forest coverages or by the side of the dancing bays. These geo-physical conditions have a profound impact on their life style and mental make-up which in course of time develop culture - sometimes these are represented as the 'crystallized form of human behaviour' and as time wears on these are handed down to posterity. It is expected that if situations or the background begin to change, then many of these core traits of culture will automatically change-specially, at the present stage, when the world has achieved progress through science and technology, through more interactions, accommodations, acculturation, enculturation, leading to changes at different degrees, sometime through conflicts and assimilations, to depict new cultural scenarios. Of course, it is believed that there are certain customs which seldom die or require plenty of background to bring about certain changes. Again, specially among so many tribal communities, we find customs in the form of laws - these envelop the groups with specific coverages and these are in vogue in many groups of so-called tribal communities.

India is a country where we find not only constrasting physical conditions but also divergent facets of population structure. There are people with distinctive language groups and as such we find variations. Whenever we speak of tribes, automatically we consider.

> A social group of simple kind, members of which speak a common language, live in common territory, have single government, sometimes act together for some common purpose, like warfare.
>
> (Riverse : 1932 : 32)

But to be more realistic we can quote Prof. T.C. Das:

> A tribe consists of groups of families who are found together by kinship, usually descending from a common mythical or legendary ancestors or who live in a common region, speak a common dialect and leave a common history. A tribe is invariably endogamous. All tribal groups which can be covered by this general definitions are not scheduled.
>
> (Das : 1953 : 246)

With reference to our country, scheduling is a constitutional privilege just to extend the facilities for overcoming the socio-economic difficulties which the groups of people face. It has been stated that in the global context tribal groups are not isolated, but the degrees of isolation vary. Changes ultimately push these groups, through interactions, acculturations and accommodations, to assimilation. There is every possibility that the dominant groups have an important role to play and as such the nature of variations is common expectation if a particular tribal group is considered. However, it is

* Total population India (1991)	...	846302688
Total tribal population (1991)	...	67758380
Total tribal population (W.B.) 1991	...	3808760

* *Excluding Jammu and Kashmir.*

an accepted fact that certain rules are not codified but are related to some groups; they cling to these rules, considering them indispensable. We accept that in many tribal communities there are uncodified laws. In this context it can be said that law may be enacted law, based on legislation, conventional law based on agreement, case law based on precedent, and customary law based on only customs. Customs reflect the norms and values of society.

II

Custom is the oldest form of law-making. Briefly speaking, custom is a continuing course of conduct observed by the community. The word 'custom' is used to apply to the totality of behaviour patterns which are continued by tradition and lodged in the group, as constructed with the more random personal activities of the individual. It is to be said that custom relates to society and law is concerned with state. In its origin customary laws appear to be only a differentiated form of general customs. The problem of the nature of customary laws is prominent in juristic theories. The two dominating modern theories are the analytical positivist school of Austin and the historical school of savigny.

'Customary law can never be complete' was the view of Brutham, the *guru* of Austin. According to Austin, law is the command of the sovereign backed by sanction. Austin says that until a custom is recognised by a court or expressed in statute it cannot become a positive law. Customs come under the rubric of positive morality. Theory of positivism treats custom as a rule of conduct which governs the society spontaneously and not as persuance of law set by any political superiors. Maine (1946) warned against the application of Austinian view as a test of customary law.

The historical school of Savigny has held customary law as a spontaneous expression of the genius of people. It arises from people's juristic consciousness when rules are regarded as legal. This school of jurisprudence claims that custom was the main vehicle of legal development. The historical school envisages that law is not made, that law is evolved from the bottom of the society, and not imposed from the top. Customary law is followed because it is convenient, conducive and helpful to the society. It reflects societal norms and values. To illustrate the idea with a simile, custom is like a 'small trodden pathway' which is formed and shaped, bearing footprints that show the uniform user.

> 'Customary law is an iron law which no tribes man would dare to oppose or evade, and yet it is not laid down or enforced by a sovereign political authority, since in vast number of tribes there is no sovereign political authority in any modern sense of the word.'—
>
> (Montmorency : 1920)

We have to accept that the individual cannot go beyond a certain point as he has to follow the rules of the society. Of course, public opinion cannot be ignored; in reality, it controls the human behaviours, though these vary in time - space dimensions. Naturally, customs consist of social norms and social norms are sanctioned by the society composed of people of varied ranks and statuses and mental attitudes. Naturally, law consists of social norms. Negative sanction can punish with a hardpelting of hateful words on a scornful curl of the lips and sometimes with many other things when things go beyond the norms or patterns of social life. Actually, we have to accept that 'law has teeth and teeth can bite'. It is also an accepted fact that

> 'Law without force is an empty name or a legal rule without coercion, is a fire that does not bury alight that does not shine.'
>
> (Hoebel and Frost : 1979)

Law practically functions to maintain the society and gradually adjusts itself with the social systems for the perpetuation as well as stability of the society. The objectives of adhering to these principles make the human groups adapt to the environment. If the environment changes, so the nature of adjustment also changes along with the laws or customs. Through these changes of custom, society tries to meet new socio-economic conditions and this is familiar in customary laws. The starting-point of custom is convention rather than conflict. It is an accepted fact that custom is perpetuated by imitation. According to many, imitation is one of the primary laws of nature. Custom is the great stabilising factor in the society. Custom may be good or bad, or both. In Indian society old invalid parents are generally looked after by the grown-up or mature sons but torturing the witches or killing them ruthlessly by beating or pelting stones is an evil custom prevalent among the Santals. This may be an example of superstition. It is an accepted fact that customs existed in society prior to the birth of courts and laws. With the gradual growth of the legal system, customs began to lose their importance. In Indian situation as a whole, customs still have importance. Burning of *Sati* and remarriage.

> Naste Mrite Prabrajite
> Klibleha Patite Patau,
> Pancha Apatsu Narinang
> Patiranya Bidhiyate.
>
> —Parashara Sanghita

This sanctions widow remarriage as per Parashara Sanghita when the husband is dead, or he stays in a far-away place or accepts *Sanyasa,* when he is impotent or has lost his sense of morality of the young widows have a profound impact in the traditional Hindu society. Marital rules are also treated as customs. Among the Santals, putting vermillion on the forehead of the woman is considered as marriage. Sexual hospitality of a married Garo woman to another Garo male is wrong and the offender is punished by the society and the woman is brought to the local council where her earnings are forcibly confiscated. This is the custom.

III

Custom has often been considered as the source of law, based on legislation; in a like manner, conventional law is based on agreement, case law based on precedent and customary law based on customs. Practically customs reflect the norms and values of the society. Origin of primitive customs is always a source of law. It has been reiterated that the customs constitute the oldest form of law-making (Atchuthen : 1985). It may be said that custom is the product of concurrent action through time. The encyclopaedia of the social sciences (1959) reiterates that 'custom is usage legitimated by tradition or a norm involving unorganised sanctions'. Anthropologists look at customs as the totality of socially-acquired behaviour patterns. Those behaviours should be supported by traditions and generally exhibited by members of the society. Customs relate to society and law is concerned with state. In its origin customary law appears to be only a differentiated form of general custom. Custom is both the course and form of law. A controversy over customary laws raged in England since Austin and the continent since the emergence of the historical school.

"Customary law can never be complete", this was the view of Bentham. (Edward Sapir : 1954). In this respect it has been said by Austin that until a custom is recognised by a court or expressed in statute, it cannot become a positive law. Of course, customs come under positive morality. Theory of positivism treats customs as rule or conduct which is observed spontaneously. This is however, not the pursuance of law set by a political superior.

Social customs grew up by a gradual process. When customs are already in operation, judicial authority adds to the sanctions of general recognition. The historical school of Savigny has held customary law as a spontaneous expression of the genius of the people. It arises from the people's juristic consciousness and posits that rules shall be regarded as legal. This school of jurisprudence claims that custom was the main vehicle of legal development. As per the historical view, we endorse that law is not made but is evolved from the bottom of the society and not imposed from the top. Savigny reiterated that a legal system is a part of culture of a people. Customary law is followed because it is convenient, conducive and helpful to the society as it reflects societal norms and values.

IV

Since the days of Maine (1921), the study of anthropology developed into a separate branch of learning. Anthropological investigations into the nature of primitive and underdeveloped systems of law are of modern origin and might be regarded as the product of historical school. Speaking by and large, anthropologists study the communities, specially the so-called tribal groups who were in general nature-based and live more or less isolation, *i.e.,* in less interaction with other groups of people who are considered to be advanced. They have observed certain practices which are in vogue among them and accepted by them as a result, the pattern or function of the law differing in time-space dimensions. Let us see what the anthropological view of customary law is. What an anthropologist recognises as a body of customary laws is simply a set of specifications of rights and duties between or among the individual members of a social system.

> If we refuse to fulfil our obligations towards others we must anticipate that others will refuse to fulfil our obligations towards us. This, from Malinowski's point of view, was the supreme sanction which led to general conformity.
>
> (Hutton : 1935)

Of course, Malinowski (1949) claims that serious transgressions against accepted social mores may lead to social ostracism. He referred to cases from Trobriand islanders in support of his contention. In this case, we can refer to Radcliffe-Brown who puts stress on the conformity of customs because society as a whole prompts the individual to do so. There is a fear of possible reprisals. Another view is that obedience rests on the reciprocity of services. Leach (1982) defines law as the customary rules of the society. He disagress on certain points with Malinowski and maintains that custom may be ambiguous and susceptible to varied interpretations.

In many tribal societies studied by the anthropologists custom is sufficient to meet their needs. Hoebel (1979) says :

> 'Law performs certain functions essential to the maintenance of all but the most simple societies these are overlapped. Custom has regularity and so does the law. Custom is sanctioned and so is the law. But the sanction of law may involve physical coercion. Law is distinguished from mere

> custom in that it endows certain selected individuals with privilege-right in applying the sanction of physical coercion if need be'.

However, it is true that when organised force steps in as a sanction and drives behind a custom, it becomes a law and institution. Custom is a traditional or indigenous system of social control. Anthropologists observe that custom derives its origin from habit or repetitive performance of a particular behaviour. Philosophy find a moral content in customs and categorises them on the basis of the standards of good or evil.

Thus to a philosopher a custom becomes a subject of normative ethics. On the other hand, it is said :

> 'Customary law can best be described as languages of interaction. (Supra note I, p. 911)

His view is that customary law offers an unwritten code of conduct followed in a social setting. Tribal or extended family is not simply a chart of do's or don'ts; it is a programme for living together. Some parts of the programme may be articulated as distinct norms imposing specially-designed sanctions. But the basic logic of customary law will continue to inhere in the system as a whole. According to many, the relationship between custom and law is basically one of contradiction, not continuity :

> 'Customs, as most anthropologist agree, is characteristic of primitive society, and laws of civilisation'. (Supra note I, p. 934)

However, law and custom co-exist. Sometimes customs exists as an exception to the general law of the land, sometimes in conformity with it and sometime codified in the body of the general law. Customs are likely to develop into traditions which are stronger than law and remain unchallenged long after the reasons for their introduction have disappeared.

The most outstanding characteristic quality of custom is that the mere fact of practice and repetition invests it with a sanctity which is often more common than reason, logic or utility.

V

In the global context we find customary law in operation at different degrees. Babylonian, Chinese, German, Anthenian, Roman, Irish laws, etc., are the examples. Maine (1888) has traced the genesis of customary laws to Greece in Homeric poems and to Indian in Sanskrit literature. If we go through the Roman *Corpus Juris Civilis* (body of civil law), a large number of customary laws found. This was announced by Emperor Justinian on February 15, 528 A.D., a few months after his accession. The customary laws of medieval Germany grew from the findings of the lay judges; doubtful cases were resolved by the adoption of a declaration as to the nature of the rule of customary law after an official enquiry by the local law-finders. The common law of England in its classical period well illustrates the conception of customary law.

A typical example has been provided by Malinowski in his famous book *Crime and Custom in Savage Society* (1940) :

'Oneday an outbreak of wailing and a great commotion told me that a death had occurred somewhere in the neighbourhood. I was informed that Kimai, a young lad of my acquaintance, of sixteen or so, had fallen from a coconut palm and killed himself ... only much later I was able to discover the real meaning of these events : the boy had committed suicide. The truth was that he had broken the rules of exogamy, the partner in his crime being his maternal cousin, the daughter of his mother's sister. This has been known and generally disapproved of, but nothing was done until the girls discarded lover, who had wanted to marry her and who felt personally injured, took the initiative. This rival threatened first to use black magic against the guilty youth, but this had not much affect. Then one evening he insulted the culprit in public, accusing him in the hearing of the whole community of incest and hurling at him certain expressions intolerable to native. For this, there was only one remedy; only one means of escape remained to the unfortunate youth. Next morning he put on festive attire and ornamentation, climbed a coconut palm and addressed the community, speaking from among the palm leaves and bidding them farewell ...

> Then he wailed aloud, as is the custom, jumped from a palm tree some sixty feet high and was filled on the spot.
>
> This is the ideal native law and in moral matters, it is easy and pleasant strictly to adhere to the ideal when judging the conduct of others or expressing an opinion about conduct in general.
>
> (pp. 77 - 78)

The role of custom in the common Anglo-American law is very important. The whole traditional element is embodied in the general body of this case-law. The customary rules of inheritance and tenure were enforced as local or special or customs in England, but they are now embedded in English or American law. In international law, the role of custom has been well recognised and customary law has been looked upon and applied as 'authoritative international usage'.

VI

Customs have been envisaged by Hindu law in the approved usage. We can interpret these in the form of *Sista* which indicates *Veda*-knower, and *Achar* which means practice. Thus *Sistachar* stands for the practices of the 'Veda-knower', automatically considered to be virtuous and learned. We generally think that standard Hindu laws and customs were practised by a group of people having a very distinct social status. They are noting but the embodiment of standarised Hindu manners and customs practised by the elite or gentry of a distinctive social status. First, law originated from the *Vedas*. Thus *Smriti* and other customs were slowly accommodated and these were also treated as the source of Hindu law—to solve the problem as to how the society should be regulated. Kings had to maintain law and order and violation of the laws was taken seriously. Practically, kings had to respect all these practices, though there might be some little variations in time-space dimensions.

The *Ramayana,* the *Mahabharata,* and many other books were treated to guide the people in the form of code of conduct. It is true that bad customs were rejected as the source of law. In the *Rgveda,* clear instructions were given to adhere to a custom. Of course, there were local variations. In the *Rgveda* it was mentioned that the observance of customary rules is necessary for our own welfare as well as for preservation and perpetuation. The *Upanishadas* insists upon the canon of antiquity, reasonableness, high degree of certainty, conformity to morality and public policy to customs. The *Smritis* contemplate the government of vast population by these customs alone and the fact that they are so governed would not detract from the general authority and antiquity of the *Smritis.*

Brihaspati, or Sukracharya were considered to be the authorities on law. Thus, it is clear that Hindu law has always been customary to a great extent. The code of Manu was in force in India, Burma and Siam—in those places there were connections through contact. According to Manu, customs which have come down by immemorial traditions and which exist among the castes, pure or mixed, are called approved usages. There were many more *Rishis* like Parasara, Devala, etc. who practically modified certain codes of conduct due to regional variations. In all the cases it was believed that the *Smritis* could not be disturbed. If we interpret the entire situation we may come to the conclusion that customary laws were found in greater proportion than the written texts of the *Smirits,* the formal law.

Hindu law of succession and inheritance ultimately got codified in the Hindu Succession Act, 1956 which was based on the 'customary law' of *Dayabhaga* and *Mitakshara* schools. Section 2 (2) of both the Hindu Succession Act, 1956 and the Hindu Marriage Act 1955 leaves open the door of tribal customary laws. There are provisions for application of non-tribal customary laws too. The custom of *Saptapadi* has been transformed into. the customary law of 'seven steps' for completion of Hindu marriage; without *Saptapadi,* the marriage is not complete. Moreover, according to the Hindu Marriage Act, 1955, divorce can only be taken from either of the spouse by way of the decree of a court. This is, however, subject to the stipulation that if the divorce is sanctioned by the custom, that will be duly recognised by law. Again, Section 3 (a) of the Hindu adoption and maintenance act recognises customs and usages.

VII

In the constitution of India, Articles 244, 244A, 371A, the fifth and sixth schedules clearly indicate the concern of the makers of the constitution to preserve and maintain the customary laws of the tribes (scheduled). The constituent assembly debates and documentary evidences in this regard may be taken into consideration. Article 371A, unequivocally lays down that no act of parliament in respect of Naga customary law shall apply to the state of Nagaland unless the Legislative Assembly of Nagaland by a resolution so decides.

While launching into a discussion specially of the fifth schedule of draft constitution on 5.9.49 Sri Lakshmi Narayan Sahu made the following observation :

> Some of the customs of the aboriginals have crept into Hinduism and some of the useful customs of the Hindu have found place in the life of aboriginals (Constituent Assembly Debates, official report 30.7.49 - 18.9.49, Delhi Lok Sabha Secretariat, pp. 983-984).

Of Course, Sri Sahu worked with the tribals of Orissa. He had deeper insight and pleaded for the protection of the customary laws of the tribes. Gopinath Bordoloi joined him and emphatically moved the resolution of preserving certain traditional institutions of AO Nagas and other hill tribes:

There are certain institutions among these hill tribals which, in my opinion, are so good that, if we want to destroy them, I consider, it is to be very wrong.

Customary law is one of the most important institutions among the tribesmen, which are helpful for good administration. Bordoloi also pointed out that one of the things which he regarded as creditable to those hilly tribes is the manner in which they settle their disputes. The system of village administration of AO Nagas is very good. Their autonomy and their institutions should be preserved, this was the plea on the floor of the constituent hall on 6.9.1949. The Santal and Mahali traditional justice system claim the same importance in the indigenous process of resolving their disputes and conflicts. Moreover, while Articles 15, 16 and 19 make it possible to legislate for special conditions of the tribes in the matter of enforcing the provisions relating to the equality of all citizens, Articles 46, 275, 330, 332, 334 and 335 also protect tribal interests. Besides, many beneficial legislations show that our legislative organs are fully conscious of the customary laws of the tribesmen. And, they provide for protection of customary laws in various social and land legislations, namely the Santal Parganas Tenancy Act, 1949, the Chhotanagpur Tenancy (Supplementary) Act, 1949, the West Bengal Land and Reforms Act, 1955, the Rajasthan Tenancy Act, 1955, the Uttar Pradesh *Zamindari* Abolition and Land Reforms Act, 1950 etc. By and large, each state has come forward with the law to protect tribal customary practices and rights. The protection of Civil Rights Act, 1955, prescribes punishment for the practice of untouchability. To achieve the constitutional goal, section 16 of the protection of civil rights act brushes aside all other laws, any custom or usage which is in conflict with the act. Denying a member of a Scheduled caste or a Scheduled tribe any customary rights of passage to a place of public resort has been made punishable under section 3 (XIV) of the Scheduled Caste and Scheduled Tribes (Prevention of Atrocities Act, 1989).

VIII

While discussing customary laws which are functioning or in operation in many tribal societies it is to be understood that the basic procedural laws of India form the code of Civil Procedure, 1908 and the code of Criminal Procedure, 1973. The makers of the procedural laws carefully protected some tribal customary laws, in the very first section of each of the aforesaid codes. Section 1. (3) of the Civil Procedure Code, 1908 lays down that the code does not extend to Nagaland and Tribal areas (sixth scheduled of the constitution) but may be applied by notification to Nagaland and tribal areas. However, for the purpose of tribes of West Bengal no special procedural law has been enacted. The Civil Procedural Code, 1908 and the Criminal Procedure Code, 1973 apply to the tribesmen and non-tribes equally. In this connection the essential of valid customs are to be noted. The various decisions of the privy council, Supreme Court of India and different High Court have already indicated that the following essential attributes constitute custom :

(i) *Antiquity :* Section 3 (A) of the Hindu marriage act, 1955 provides that custom should be observed for a long time. It should be ancient. The courts have time and again held that if a custom is established to be 100 years old or more it may be treated as antiquity.

(ii) *Continuity :* It is as essential as antiquity. Discontinuity will destroy a custom. An obsolete law will destroy a custom.

(iii) *Certainty :* Custom must be certain and clear, not vague. One has to prove what exactly the custom is and how far it is applicable with a reasonable amount of certainty. A vague proposition that divorce by mutual consent is allowed on the basis of customary law is not sufficient. It has to be established that the applied custom exists.

(iv) *Reasonability :* It has a social value. It varies from time to time from place to place. An unreasonable custom is void, although custom may not be always founded on reason.

(v) *Morality :* An immoral custom is void. Like the standard of morality. Custom may differ from time to time and from society to society.

(vi) *Not opposed by public policy :* A custom opposed to public policy is void.

(vii) Custom should not be opposed to law.

We, of course, have to realise that custom is the lifeblood in the tribal societies. Tribals cannot be separated from the customary laws. It is ingrained in their life and culture so much so that any violation of the customary laws may lead to serious consequences. From the time of the birth of a child, till his death, i.e., through his entire life-cycle, there are several customary laws that must be followed. Any breach of customary laws is a subject matter of dispute in a tribal society, from which many consequences may ensure.

IX

A few events which are related to Santal customary laws have already been referred to in this dissertation and these engage the attention of the common people as well as of the scholars. These are recorded here just to pinpoint the gravity of the situation.

Sometime in April 1995 Ananda Bazar Patrika reported the case of one Budhni, a Santal woman who happend to garland Late Prime Minister Pandit Nehru at the time of the D.V.C. Dam inauguration about 40 years ago. The event reflects how Budhni, a sweet girl, approximately aged 10 years, came with her mother to work in the Dam from a village in Purulia. The organisers constructed a circular concrete platform for this purpose, where after switching on, the ceremonial inauguration was to be held by the then Prime Minister. The organisers selected Budhni for the ceremony to garland Late Prime Minister as she belonged to a tribe and the girl unhesitatingly agreed. At the time of celebration, amidst the rejoicing cheer, Budhni garlanded Prime Minister who with his usual courtesy returned the garland to the neck of Budhni, the Santal girl, before the excited crowd the celebration ended but a few elderly Santals murmured to Budhni 'Your marriage is over, so you will never be in a position to marry any one'. Thus tragedy be fell her life. She had to remain neglected, unmarried, uncared for and looked down upon by her fellow community members. She was considered a woman refused to have a husband. Days rolled on, and slowly Budhni passed her youth and lost her beauty. At last she, as an alternative, got in touch with a Bengali youth who happened to work in a mine. After a few years her Bengali lover lost his job due to a strike in the quarry. They all people had to starve and they were not to get any opportunity or any alternative and ultimately some one instructed Budhni and her consort to appeal to the then Prime Minister Rajeev Gandhi who realised the situation and arranged to offer them jobs in a nearby mine. Now Budhni does not belong to the Santal community. She is permanently ostracized by the Santal society. We are to see how this customary law is operating in the society.

Another very painful tragic instance was published in almost all the daily papers regarding the merciless killing of one Santal woman, Tamali and her second husband, a Hindu youngman named Shakti Kundu. Earlier, Tamali married a Santal boy, but they were not technically divorced. In respect of divorce a *Sal* leaf was to be torn perfectly and straight, otherwise it would not be accepted by the society. In this case, the Manjhis from two village did not come and assemble to see the tearing of the *Sal* leaf. This leaf was to be torn into two pieces. It was not done in the case of Tamali. So it was not treated as a divorce by the Santal society. Naturally, the whole society took the matter in a different way. Violation of such procedures is seriously treated. In such cases, two persons, male and female, are to be slashed. As per the Santal dictionary, it is 'Mak', meaning :

> to slash, hack, chop, hew, slash, cut off, beheaded, decapitate, etc.

As a result, both the persons Tamali, the Santal girl, and the Hindu boy were chopped off by the angry mob and thrown near their hut. This sort of activity, as per the Santal customary law, is proper and justified. Before that incident, Tamali married twice. Her first marriage was with a Santal boy. But the members of Tamali's family did not approve of this marriage which ultimately led the couple to seek divorce. Her second marriage took place with another boy. Radhu Murmu, but they were not technically divorced as nobody used to stay separately. At that time Saktipada (who was chopped off by the Santal society) fell in love with Tamali and then the incident took place. Naturally, it is very difficult to violate customary laws by the Santals as these are obligatory and form part of the social system.

One I.P.S. police officer Mr. A.B. Choudhury has published a book in Bengali entitled: *'Santal Samaj Daini O Bartaman Sankat* (Kolkata : 1985), i.e., the *Santal Society, Witch and the Present-day Crisis*. As a topranking police officer he has clearly interpreted many ruthless killings of the Santal witches who were suspected by the society and endorsed by the *Jan guru*, the person who can foretell the events. The activities of the witches are generally related to epidemic, death of the babies or any continued suffering of a different nature. These are first reported to the priest and he advises the reporters to consult the *Janguru* who is to suggest the remedial measures. The suggestion is tantamount, in the truest sense, to ruthless killing of a suspected witch - who is identified by the *Janguru*. Mr. Choudhury has described many events in true perspectives. If any epidemic starts in a village, then the timid villagers rush to the *Janguru* who can foresee and fore tell the future regarding the causes of the event. In most of the cases failure to detect a proper cause is attributed to someone and this leads to the diagnosis of the cauge in a person who will be killed as per the prevailing custom of the Santal society. So these killings or murders are not considered harmful in the Santal society; rather they are unavoidable step for the perpetuation of the society. This faith is deep-rooted among the Santals.

Thus, we are to accept that customs approve of these ruthless killings and that nobody is considered to be guilty such killings. This is a way of reflection of the Santal Customary law and this has no scientific explanation. Generally, uncouth, badlooking persons or the childless widows or widowers are suspected by the *Janguru*. Thus we see how a custom becomes deep-rooted.

In reality, sanctity of customs among the tribals is great. Thus the role of customary law in the tribal society is highly significant. In actual sense, codified laws or statutes exclude the tribal customary laws. It can be said that customary laws in the so-called tribal society can be termed means of social control.

X

Study of the functioning of customary laws of the tribal communities is very important as the so-called tribal communities (numbering about 500) at different parts of this country have distinctive life-styles due to various techno-ecosystems. After independence many ameliorative programmes on the part of the government have been launched to the tribals and for even those who are considered to be most backward a new administrative term, P.T.G. (Primitive Tribal Group), has been used just to give them more advantages and benefits on the basis of which they can stand on their own feet and overcome the age-old difficulties. It is true that almost all the tribal societies have distinct ways of life, values and belief-systems. As human beings, they also face many more problems, when they confront divergent situations. It is, of course, an undeniable fact that we may disapprove many more things of their culture, but in fact they try to adjust themselves with different situations only to eke-out their existence and to have a peaceful life by maintaining a social order. Sometimes elderly persons have to play a dominant role, to settle many disputes or disorders. In many situations, we have to accept that this totality of behaviour patterns is ultimately accepted by the groups and these are handed down to posterity. In this way, gradual crystalizations of the group mentality, rather the habits, incomprehensible or tantalizing or exotic, are being displayed into the systematic process, and ultimately grouping these into larger configurations which have formal cohesion, all these, in course of time, tend to rationalise through some functional units of behaviour. All these again, in course of time,. tend to rationalise through some functional units of behaviour reflecting varied degrees of conservation in regard to customs. In the truest sense these bear the evidence of psychological compulsion of law which is controlled by the society through imposition of exclusive penalties; these may be called ethics or more primitively 'mores'. It is, of course, assumed that mundane or human sovereignty becomes progressively distinguished from socially-diffused or supernatural or impersonal sovereignty. In this way, customary laws become a spontaneous expression of the genius of the people, arising from their juristic consciousness and determining subjectively when rules shall be regarded as legal. We have to accept that custom does not become law until it acquires a clear and definite sanction. It is also accepted that in the early system of law, sanctions are often imperfect and informal. We have to accept that the customs come to be accompanied by some ceremonials, borrowed no doubt from religious rituals, but really differentiating the transactions as creating relations on an obligatory or formal characteristic of customary law that implies that the availability of judges is more important than the availability of the settled rules of the law. The right of judgement has to be vested in some persons or class of persons e.g., priestly or comparatively aristocratic class. Customary law, then, represents the intermediary stage in judicial evolution when law has ceased to be conceived simply as the will of the gods (Hindu *Dharma*) and as entailing divine displeasure. An additional sanction has been found in the fact that judgements are supposed to derive their force from the existence of popular customs. Thus, customary laws are an expression of the genius of a whole people.

In this connection it can be said that customs of contiguous or afflicted tribes are likely to be similar, atleast in the broader aspects of the political union of the tribes. Thus these attest to the primitive form of positive law flourished as unwritten law and continue to play a more supplementary part in the adjustment of local interests, indicating that unwritten law which usage has approved. It has been said that old legal customs sometimes postulated that where no statute was directly applicable, local custom should be applied. Thus, we find, old types of land tenures and some varieties of incidents have survived in this way among many groups of tribes. However, almost all the tribal communities are chained with the customary laws which are unwritten and not formally codified by the general law. The nature of social offences, crime, tort or sin, are realised by the groups concerned and as such alternative prohibitive measures are outlined and accepted by the groups concerned. Penalties vary from group to group as the understanding and realisation differ through enveloping cultural or traditional reflections. However, in general, it can be said that the customary law of a tribe is built upon the nature of experience as well as for perpetuation in meeting new circumstances as they arise. Change in customary law, of course, takes place owing to new conditions of life superimposed on the people by outside influence or political governance which creates new legal possibilities and through the radical shifts of basic principles due to accelerated modernisation and rapid interaction through varied nation-building processes. Sometimes among migrant or dispersed tribal groups the central authority does not exist and in that sense kinship-group plays an important role for law and order and in jurisprudence.

XI

Attempts have been made in this dissertation to peep into the details of the functioning customary laws as prevalent in some tribal groups of West Bengal with special reference to the Bengal-Bihar-Orissa border. It is important to note that the Austric-speaking tribes, the Santals are considered to be the main group. Other allied groups are Mahali, Kheria, Kora, Munda, Bhumij and the Lodhas. Of course, after fifty years of independence many more changes have taken place in their socio-political as well as economic life, specially in West Bengal where a popular government is ruling the state and the government, by establishing Panchayati Raj, has given more power to the down-trodden people along with other local people who were once lagging behind. We have attempted here to show how far after getting all these benefits the groups of people still adhere to the traditional customs where customary laws play a dominant role in guiding the society. In one sense, traditional customary laws might have been set aside due to the spread of education or due to the new political power-structure when people's representation through democratic election has been established. The political party in power has been ruling the state for more than twenty years.

Tribal population and the background of the informants have been described in chapter two. However, the Santals are treated as the great *Hor* race. The word *Hor* means man. The Santals call themselves *Hor* and the others are considered as *Diku*, i.e., 'outsider', or alien. It is important to note here that the Mahalis are practically bamboo-workers and the Koras are 'earth workers'. As per the Santal tradition they are low in status. The Kherias are regarded as a non-agricultural community. Then come the Mundas - most of them have migrated from the Chotanagpur plateau and gradually made their dwelling place in various parts of this state. The Bhumijes and the Lodhas are almost Hinduised and they have forgotton their own language and accepted local Bengali - but the nature of pronounciation varies from place to place. It is indicated that in many of their social customs local Hindu traits reveal themselves in varied degrees. Naturally, our attempt is to see how far customary laws dominate or gradually fade away, and what the causes of losing its strength appear to be.

Once the Ministry of Welfare (T.D.) became interested in studying the 'customary laws' of the tribal communities with the following objectives :

(1) The Customary tribal laws once known and codified will throw light on the inter-relationship among

the members of the tribal community, particularly so far as the administration of affairs of the tribal society is concerned.

(2) Land and property laws once known may reduce litigation to a considerable extent if the customary role of the tribal institutions in the concerned sphere is activised.

Of course, in this regard some studies have been undertaken and specially the Law Research Institute for the eastern region, Gauhati, has done some work on the tribal customs. A few research institutes as well as the Anthropological Survey of India have completed some projects which may be of use for the administration. Besides, the state government of West Bengal has a special Scheduled Castes and Scheduled Tribes Welfare Department in every district. It has one officer to overcome problems and difficulties; the officers are to help the contending parties in respect of setting disputes. Against such a background this study adopts an empirical view to understand tribal problems on the one hand and to postulate a better mode of administration on the other.

Thrust is here given on how far the *Panchayati Raj* government, in course of their twenty years' rule in a progressive way with many political promises, have been able to change the obstinate tribal culture - which might not be considered as scientific. In this connection, an attempt has been made to study the tribal groups mentioned before - to investigate how far they are involving themselves in the nation-building processes.

With this idea, we have tried to study the functioning of the customary laws which possibly once dominated the life-pattern of the tribal groups. Our objective is also to examine how far these are operating or gradually fading away due to urbanisation, spread of education, new employment facilities or changed political faith or ideology which have enveloped their mind and action-pattern. Again, we have tried to explain or ascertain why or how these groups of people have to shift their own habitat to a new setting along with other groups of people having an impact on their life-style and world-view.

In this context, it is to be noted that man's adaptation process is continuing all the time, but if the locale is changed, if social cohesion with other groups of people extends, then many of the older customs are sure to change. Naturally, this study indicates the nature of shifting from one point to other and shows how non-traditional mentality is being transplanted into the minds of the people. In this connection, it is to be observed that the pressure of population, specially on the land, has been gradually increasing and as such movement of the people has become both common and regular. It is expected that many more changes in respect of the prevailing views of the customary laws are sure to occur with the rule of the ruling political party in this state.

XII

It has been stated that a systematic study of the customary laws started long ago, specially in India. British administrators, while facing considerable unrest among the so-called tribals, did not disturb them. As a result, enquiries were made as to how customary laws operated in many tribal societies. Many more administrators, missionary people and scholars took a special interest in the matter. Rev. L.D. Skrefarud was the first person to document the Santal traditions. P.O. Bodding translated the book entitled *Horkorean Mare Hapraneko Reak Katha* (traditions and institutions of the Santals). Rev. Skrifsrud wrote the book in 1887 in

Santalee. Bodding reedited the book in 1916 and 1929. This book gives a vivid account of many Santal traditions and customs. It is written on the ethnographical aspect of the tribe in which the legal angle is missing. An important area of customary law, i.e., civil and criminal justice system from village to pargana does not find its proper place even in Bodding's book.

The main findings of Bodding are :

(i) There are phases of development in Santal customary laws.

(ii) There are borrowings from Aryan sources but a considerable portion indicates their Santal origin.

(iii) After prolonged contacts and deliberations the Santals abondoned some of their own customs and adopted Hindu practices instead.

However, Santal customary laws have been studied by some other distinguished scholars. W.B. Archer deserves special mention. His book was first published in 1984 and was again edited by K.S. Singh. Archer (1907-79) was an administrator (1931–1946). He utilised his career in the rural areas of Bihar (in many districts of Bihar) and became interested in studying the tribal life in general but the customary laws of the Santals in particular. As Deputy Commissioner of Santal Parganas (December 1942 - June 1945) he came in contact with the tribesmen. Many more conflict cases were finalised and as such he was in a better position to understand the Santal customary laws. He realised that custom is only a part of tribal laws. Tribal law in fact is a set of principles - which a tribe accepts and applies. Archer's activities are limited to his administrative jurisdiction, i.e., within the Santal Parganas. According to him.

> 'It is an attempt to record Santal law at a certain time and in certain place'.

Of course, he referred to Dalton, Grigson, Haimendorf, Elwin, Campbell, Roy and Bompus, the renowned authors of Indian tribal ethnography, who recorded laws and mentioned customs in detail. One of the advantages on the part of Archer, was that he knew the Santal language which helped him to understand tribal problems in a true perspective.

Ethnographers rendered a lot of half to the administration. Practically they were in a position to steer clear of the difficulties which the administrators faced; their purpose was just to help the administration peacefully. Late J.K. Bose was possibly the first anthropologist who studied the Garo Law of inheritance. The then Settlement Officer faced difficulties while trying to solve the problem of land settlement in the Garo areas of Mymansingh. As the group of people are matriarchate, automatically land and properties are handed down from mother to daughters. The youngest daughter i.e., *Nokna,* she inherits the residential home where her parents stay. Many more financial duties are being performed by her. So the Garo law of inheritance was published (1941) by the University of Calcutta as a valuable authentic report on the Garo customs. As the Garos are matriarchate, the Settlement Officer faced problems in land settlement and tenure. J.K. Bose was invited to investigate and to collect information in respect of the conflicting situations which enabled him to record and publish his findings in the book form. Hajra has elaborated the customary laws of the Kolams of Maharastra. Elwin describes many more tribes of which the Saoras of Orissa are very important. North-eastern tribes' customary laws were described by Kusum and Bakshi. In this connection it can be said that customary laws regarding divorce, maintenance, inheritance, adoption and guardianship have been duly considered by the authors. The custom of divorce and the laws of inheritance among the Khasis have been dealt with by a Bre (1964). Arunachal Pradesh tribes have been studied and more emphasis has been laid on the Wanhos. (The Law Research Institute, Gauhati High Court, 1981).

Of course, in 1979 Goswami edited another book on the customary laws of the Mizos. Goswami also conducted a study on 'Tripuri and Tripura'. This book covers interalia customary laws relating to marriage, divorce, adoption, maintenance, succession and inheritance. Roy and Rizvi dealt with the customary laws of the Nagas, Garos and Mizos in their book 'Tribal Customary Laws of North East India, (1990). Bhowmick's restudy of the Chenchus (1992) clearly explains the customary laws of the Chenchus of Andhra Pradesh. Elwin's further study touched upon the Muria life. Rai and Vidyarthi described many more customary laws very lucidly, though their materials have been collected from different authors. Chhattisgarh district has been covered by the scholars of Anthropological Survey of India. Elwin's detailed descriptions of the Angami Nagas are notable. Andamanese life has been described by Radcliffe Brown (1922). Bajpayee (1995) portrayed the customs and rituals of the Buddhist tribes of Lahul-spiti, Himachal Pradesh.

Recently some books have come out in respect of the customary laws of some groups of people in different parts of our country. Raghavia described many cases in his book *Tribal Justice* (1968). Bose, in *Glimpses of Tribal life in North-East India* (1980), discussed many customs of the tribal groups of North East India. He wrote about the dual organisation in Assam, Tri-clan and marriage classes, Nokrom system of the Garos and Garo-law of inheritance. Roy and Rizvi (1990) discussed in detail the tribal customary laws of north-east India. Bhatia (1991) edited Law and Social Action, where we can get some examples by different authors from different parts of our country. One recent publication entitled *Tribal Ethnography, Customary Law and Change,* edited by K.S. Singh (1993), includes some interesting papers by different writers. This book, in its aims and scope, practically almost ranges over the whole of India and can be accepted as one of the most updated books so far published.

XIII

In order to get information in respect of the 'Customary Laws' of some Austric-speaking people attempts have been made to study some tribes having different systems of economy as well as habitats. Above all, three frontier districts, Purulia, Bankura and Midnapur, have been selected; so have been the tribes, namely, Santal, Mahali, Kora, Kheria, Munda, Bhumij and Lodha living in different areas. The case histories of these tribes have been recorded. Many of their traditional customs, referred to in their own panchayat or tackled by the local panchayats or in the respective courts, have also been mentioned.

Some villages, exclusively inhabited by a particular tribe, and some others by other tribals as well as caste groups, have been selected to collect all requisite information. The field work was conducted by senior scholars who stayed in the field, used proforma and collected information accordingly. It is to be noted that this state is ruled by the Left Front Ministry headed by CPI (M) who have a progressive political view and who endorse the *Panchayati Raj,* where members of the panchayat are being elected by adult franchise. Naturally, many older views might have been diluted an have faded out. Beside this, our state government engaged law officers in respective district offices in the

Department of Scheduled Caste and Scheduled Tribe welfare to deal with the affairs of administration more scientifically. The research findings are placed here systematically along with the cases dealt with in the courts and government departments.

Chapter Two

THE SETTING

I

The main thrust of this dissertation is to examine the functioning of the customary laws as prevalent among some Austric-speaking tribal people of frontier Bengal where the tribal people live from hoary past interacting with nature as well as with other groups of people who are more or less in a pristine state. As such, the frontier tract of West Bengal is here considered appropriate for this study because we see a good many autochthonous tribal people among whom customary laws might be in existence. At the same time, this region is more or less a rugged terrain with occasional undulations, sometimes covered with thick jungles, but in many places they have become thinner due to the marathon axing of the people who survive with so many pressures of stress and strain. After fifty years of independence, some welfare activities have been initiated and these may have changed the life-style as well as the mental make up of the progeny of the autochthonous group of people. They are actually treated as the early settlers. In the truest sense, these so called tribal communities are accommodating themselves with the shifting scenarios and socio-political upheavals and all these, taken together, have brought about many other changes in the social mental aspects of these groups of people due to new types of interactions. Many more tribal people are in an advantageous position not only to enjoy the constitutional facilities but also to utilise the resources of nature in which they are anchored, as the hill and jungle environment has guaranteed them isolation as well as security. These interactions have undoubtedly changed their social setting and mentality, and it is expected that many more traditional, age-old modes of thinking as well as activities are in a weaning stage. After independence more emphasis has been laid on adult franchise just to elect their representatives to administer the society. Such democratic views are gradually galvanising the age-old traditions. So there might be a question; how far these traditional attitudes operate to maintain and govern the society? But, we have to believe that certain customs seldom die— though many more processes of modernisation are in operation, the age-old customary laws are mostly observed. Naturally, this location has been chosen for the present type of study. This zone is a virgin area where these autochthonese groups of people have lived for several centuries together; at the same time, welfare activities through more radical political parties are being carried on. Even the views of the elderly people are accepted with esteem. Thus, this zone has been selected for this study, specially to examine the functioning of the customary laws. Industrialization processes are in operation— new views of science and technology are slowly penetrating with the interaction of their old ideas, just to bring about a change. Due to all these factors, old views and ideas are expected to change and new views will be built through various political involvements. So this tract of land has been selected for this type of study.

II

Geographical settings of the three districts, Purulia, Bankura and Midnapur, have been considered to be a part of frontier Bengal. Lateritic undulations of different intensity, sometimes covered with patches of vegetation, are visible. Sometimes dwarf *sal* and *mahua* and many other trees grow just to guarantee the living of the tribals. We may also expect various wild animals; occasional inroads of elephants are common in this area. There are a few rivers and rivulets which become dry in scorching summer, but and in the rainy season these become unfordable. All these provide shelter to the so-called autochthonous communities who undoubtedly claim their old status. We have evidence of stone-age tools possibly used by the gatherer-hunter people of bygone ages. Again, we find polished stone tools in some places and these suggest the beginning of agriculture. In course of time, almost all these groups of people might have spread to other areas, indicating this tract as the homeland of early settlers. Table 2.1 details the tribal population in three districts under study.

Table 2.1

Tribal population (1981)

	Districts	*1991*	*1981*
1.	Purulia	4,27,766	3,48,375
2.	Bankura	2,89,906	2,50,590
3.	Midnapur	6,89,636	5,43,784
	Total Tribal Population (W.B.)	38,08,760	30,70,672
	Total Population (W.B.)	6,80,77,965	5,45,80,647

It is important to note that these three districts harboured the following tribal (major) communities.

Table 2.2

Major tribal groups and the districts

Purulia	... Oraon, Kora, Bedia, Bhumij, Munda, Kheria, Santal, etc.
Bankura	... Oraon, Kora, Bhumij, Mahali, Munda, Kheria, Santal, etc.
Midnapur	... Oraon, Kora, Bhumij, Mahali, Lodha, Kheria, Santal, etc.

There are a few minor tribal groups. But for our purposes, i.e., for the study of functioning customary laws, Oraon has been omitted as this tribal community belongs to the Dravidian-speaking tribe. The greatest importance has been attached to the Austric-speaking tribes, i.e., (1) Santal, (2) Kora, (3) Mahali, (4) Kheria, (5) Munda, (6) Bhumij and (7) Lodha. But, in the truest sense, customary laws generally dominate among the Santals as they are more conservative, though Christianity has tilted their age-old views.

Table 2.3

Details population size

Sl. No.	*Districts*	*Population (1981)*			
1.	Purulia	Santal	(1,24,097)	Kora	(17,915)
		Bhumij	(73,183)	Kheria	(1,017)
		Munda	(6,662)	Mahali	(5,816)
2.	Bankura	Santal	(2,08,296)	Kora	(8,364)
		Mahali	(1,472)	Kheria	(283)
		Munda	(1,157)	Bhumij	(27,225)

3.	Midnapur	Santal	(2,55,322)	Kora	(17,795)
		Mahali	(8,586)	Kheria	(16,534)
		Munda	(33,238)	Bhumij	(7,887)
			Lodha (30,000) (As per Lodha Dev. Cell)		

*In census report Lodha/Kheria/Savar are mixed together and we get a figure 16,534 which is doubtful.

III

Against this background the following villages have been studied. It is to be noted that altogether 10+32+48=90 villages have been covered, where the tribals dominate, and some cases have been reported.

Table 2.4
Villages Studied
(District-wise)

Sl. No.	*Name of the Districts*	*Name of the Village*
1.	Purulia	(1) Herbona (2) Golkiddi (3) Rangathani (4) Biskudra (5) Pathormora (6) Borthhoria (7) Kutra (8) Chowkan (9) Malian (10) Rajnoagash Cahnda.
2.	Bankura	(1) Rajgora (2) Bantilla (3) Jamshedpur (4) Rupahir (5) Tatulchita (6) Guanala (7) Bansnala (8) Jhilimili (9) Rautora (10) Bansphari (11) Muchikata (12) Gulpura (13) Haramghari (14) Tilabani (15) Charku (16) Ramnagar (17) Pakakula (18) Tilaki (19) Bhalukunia (20) Khasia (21) Bansdiha (22) Barmetala (23) Khayerpahari (24) Bandarkhonda (25) Bhuyari (26) Bhasudanga (27) Saranga (28) Valluckchora (29)

		Jalhari (30) Barda (31) Mukutmanipur (32) Bansnala.
3.	Midnapur	(1) Tala (2) Murakata (3) Chatnasole (4) Binayee (5) Susinda (6)Ghotnagar (7) Achbar (8) Jathia (9) Gidhini (10) Charichaka (11) Chadabhila (12) Birjatsla (13) Pilagaria (14) Nawagon (15) Sahari (16) Khudmari (17)Pichaboni (18) Chakjati (19) Bargopal (20) Pathuria (21) Dhuliacha (22) Gaganeswar (23) Sindhurgoura (24) Sargaria (25) Lotanpara (26) Noapukur (27) Barbaria (28) Hatibandh (29) Kamarchowki (30) Bolarabati Kali (31) Sekharpari (32) Maynapara (33) Belti (34) Aguibani (35) Chakmakrampur (36) Chtomadakpur (37) Sarisa (38) Sijua (39) Basudevpur (40) Bastalapur (41) Bhadrakali (42) Kotaigarh (43) Kajla (44) Bankatola (45) Daharpur (46) Birkarh (47) Padampur (48) Banpatna.

For our purposes only the cases related to customary laws have been enquired; explorations have been made of the nature of functioning or violating customary laws. In case of violation special emphasis has been placed on the nature of authority. For social control has to be accepted by the parties concerned in dispute; therefore, provisions have to be forced on them if anybody protests or resists. At the same time, emphasis has been given to the mechanism of dispute management, because law has tooth and it can bite.

With all these views only the cases or nature of disputes have been recorded, we have also examined how far these are in tune with traditional formalities among the groups without much protest.

IV

Communities examined

First, the cases of the Santal have already been examined because the Santals show the elaborate examples of customary laws even today. The group of people are settled agriculturists and live in finely-knit social organisation and elaborate class system. Many more formalities are performed by the group. But those who have embraced Christianity have been avoided. Some scholars worked and they elaborately studied the group and as such some publications are available about this tribe. Next, come the Mahilas - who are linguistically the Austro-Asiatic group, like the Santals. They are considered one of the off shoots of the Santals. In order to prepare bamboo baskets, they have specialised in basket work as caste occupation model. It has been stated that *Mah* in Santali means *Bamboo*. They are also distributed in the frontier districts. A few scholars have already worked among them as regards their ethonographic identity. Next come the Koras - they belong to the Austric group of people, in language as well as in custom. The Koras have been studied by very few scholars. They are like the Santals, patriarchate people, and are distributed in the frontier districts. The next community studied for the purpose of customary laws is the Kheria. Though they are an Austro-Asiatic speaking tribe, they are not settled agriculturists. They have an elaborate clan organisation and economically they are not well-off. This group of people are distributed in these three frontier districts. Some scholars have conducted field work among this group of people and there are few books and papers written about them.

Next, the author has considered the case of the Mundas. They were basically from the Chhotanagpur plateau and in course of their migration they settled at various places of West Bengal. They have an elaborate clan organisation and they live in clusters of villages where they adjust themselves with varied groups of people. The next tribe considered is the Bhumij. The Bhumij people are considered none but the Mundas, but in course of time they have lost their own language. They are patriarchate and settled agriculturists. They are also distributed in this state specially in three frontier districts. The next group studied are the Lodhas. They have not their own language possibly due to rapid Hinduisation; like the Bhumij, they have to accept many more Hindu customs and traits but they are still identified because of their special features. It is to remembered that the Lodhas are in most cases landless, though they live in villages, having elaborate networks of organisation, but none of them are found to embrace Christianity as do the Santals, Mundas and Mahalis. Anyway, details of the study areas have been reflected in Table 2.5.

Table 2.5

Districts and the Tribes

(As per Census 1981)

Sl. No.	*Tribes*	*Purulia*	*Bankura*	*Midnapur*
1.	Santal	124097	208296	255322
2.	Mahali	5816	1472	8586
3.	Kora	17915	8364	17795
4.	Kheria/Lodha	1017	283	16534
5.	Munda	6662	1157	33238
6.	Bhumij	73183	27225	7887
7.	Lodha*	-	-	30000

*After Lodha cell enumeration.

However, for our purposes the requisite number of families have been studied to note the functioning of customary laws. Ambiguous cases have been avoided. But in all these cases attempts have been made to ascertain how far traditional customary laws are in operation and how far they react and to see how far elected members or the panchayat have handed the problems during the last 20 years of democratic representation to govern the society. Thus changes are dominant.

Informants, as mentioned, are selected not only from one district but from three districts. At the same time, no complete village enumeration has been done; only the persons involved in the situation or those who are involved in respect of operation of customary laws have been interrogated only 350 persons (rather families) have been studied and information from them have been recorded and elaborated, while finalising actualities. Table 2.6 elaborates the distribution of the families.

Table 2.6

Distribution of tribal groups

Sl. no.	*Tribes*	*Purulia*	*Bankura*	*Midnapur*	*Total*
1.	Santal	18	32	44	94
2.	Mahali	21	13	14	48
3.	Kora	17	11	11	39
4.	Kheria	16	16	7	39
5.	Munda	30	-	16	46
6.	Bhumij	22	16	22	60
7.	Lodha	-	-	24	24
					350

It can be mentioned here that only 350 (persons/families) were enquired in three districts for 7 different tribal groups. This person/families provide a general picture in respect of customary laws prevailing among the tribal groups mentioned earlier. It is believed that an enquiry into the problem will reflect the prevailing view among the tribal groups of this region.

The demographic picture of the informants has been given. It reveals that out of 350 families belonging to all the aforementioned tribal communities the total number of individuals is 1655 of which 47.55 per cent are unmarried, whereas 44.76 per cent are married. Numbers of widows/widowers revealed in percentage are 7.98. This population structure in seven tribal groups practically reflects the sample number which has been pinpointed in our research design.

Just to get an idea of the family composition of all these tribes, we may use the following Table 2.7.

However, with all these background material the report in the book form has been prepared. We presume that the information in the form of report will depict an overview of the situation.

Use of proforma, case histories and personal observations have been incorporated in the following pages of this ethnograph just to get a clear picture of the situation.

Table 2.7

Family composition

Family composition	*1 Santal 94*	*2 Mahali 48*	*3 Kora 39*	*4 Kheria 39*	*5 Munda 46*	*6 Bhumij .60*	*7 Lodha 24*	*Total 350*
Husband, Wife, Unmarried Children	61	29	21	23	28	26	20	-
Husband, Wife, Married Son with Wife	18	14	11	7	9	24	-	-
Husband, Wife, Married Sons with Children	3	1	2	3	3	3	-	-
Husband, Wife, Unmarried Brother	7	1	-	-	2	3	-	-
Broken family, widow no children	5	3	5	6	4	4	4	-
Total	94	48	39	39	46	60	24	350

Table 2.8

Land holding

Area in bigha	*1*	*2*	*3*	*4*	*5*	*6*	*7*
	Santal	*Mahali*	*Kòra*	*Kheria*	*Munda*	*Bhumij*	*Lodha*
(.54 Dec.)	*98*	*48*	*39*	*39*	*46*	*60*	*24*
No Land	11	16	08	17	03	04	04
0 - 5	54	31	24	18	33	36	19
6 - 9	22	01	06	03	03	13	01
10 - 14	06	-	01	01	04	04	-
15 - 19	01	-	-	-	03	03	-
Total families	94	48	39	39	46	60	24

Chapter Three

TRIBAL PANORAMA

I

Tribal communities of India have some obscure past and in many cases it is mixed with myths and unbelievable events. Referring to these we may postulate something on the basis of which we reconstruct their possible past history as a means to the discovery of truth. Under such circumstances we find myths and mythology, some colourful, incredible events, and ultimately we find them handed down to posterity. It is true that the tribal communities had to move from one place to another for security and peaceful life and in circumstantial exigencies they had to adopt new ways of life. Still many of their pristine habits are not missing. These are reflected in the form of legends, tales and usages.

This tract of India, almost co-terminous with Bengal (West Bengal), Bihar, Orissa and Madhya Pradesh, has a similar ecology and way of life, though the states differ in situational contexts. The groups of people in this forest region have reclaimed patches of land owing to extension of family and thus they are in a position to establish villages. Other groups of scheming communities penetrated and occupied the land, thanks to their superior technology. In course of time the so-called autochthonese groups of people were pushed into the abysmal depth of poverty and had to face difficulties.

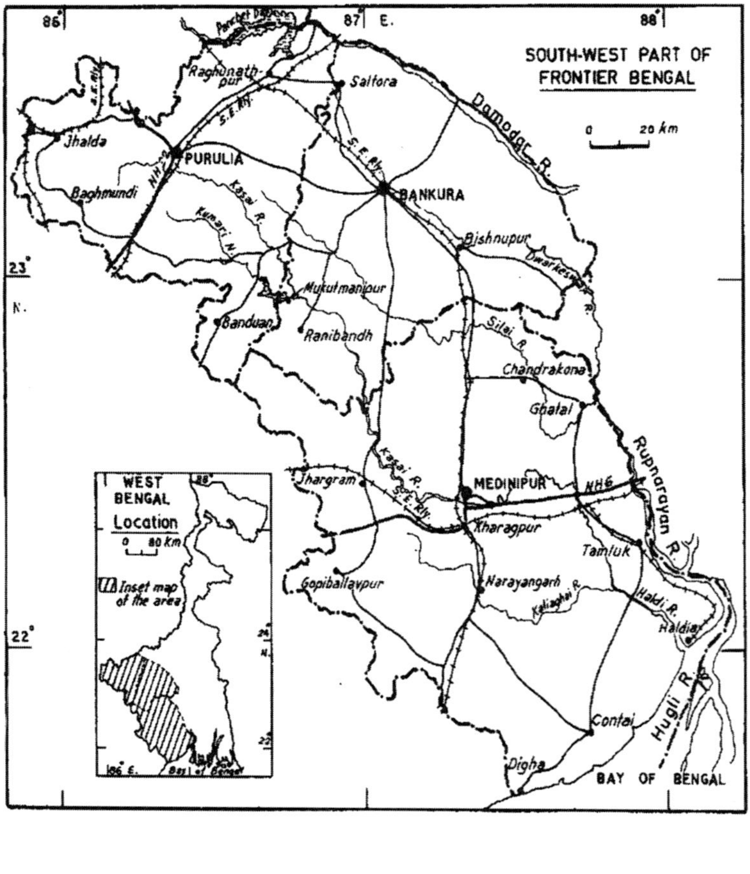
SOUTH-WEST PART OF
FRONTIER BENGAL
0 20 km
86°
87° E.
88°
23°
N.
22°
Raghunathpur
Saltora
Jhalda
PURULIA
Baghmundi
BANKURA
Damodar R.
S.E. Rly.
Kasai R.
Kumari N.
Bishnupur
Dwarkeswar R.
Mukutmanipur
Banduan
Ranibandh
Silai R.
Chandrakona
Ghatal
Rupnarayan R.
MEDINIPUR
NH6
Jhargram
Kharagpur
Tamluk
Gopiballavpur
Narayangarh
Kaliaghai R.
Haldi R.
Haldia
Hugli R.
Contai
Digha
BAY OF BENGAL
WEST
BENGAL
Location
0 80 Km
Inset map
of the area
86° E.
Bay of Bengal

This is the past history of many more tribal communities in India.

In the present context, we find that the major tribal groups are the Santals and their off shoots. It is postulated that these groups of people might have penetrated to this tract from the south-east (Agneya) and were hence known as *Agneya.* They speak a different dialect and their dialect has little similarity with that of the following groups of people. Nevertheless, we may reconstruct of postulate their past history thus :

Austric

(a)	(b)	(c)	(d)	(e)
Austro-Asiatic Koli, Santal, Munda, Ho, Kora-Bhumij, Kheria, Juang etc.	Monkh-mor (Indo-China strain)	Khasia	Nicobarese Malay Peninsula	Austro-nacian

However, we have to be very particular in using the terms which can be scientifically accepted. We must accept that the use of the term Austric is not scientifically correct as per the linguistic classification of these groups of people. Suniti Kumar (1928) prefers to apply the term *Kol* to the groups which we are to discuss. Many more legends have been placed and accommodated to depict their early history. Sometimes along with the myths and mythology, the *Puranas* and other books mention all these in order to enliven the realities and as such a very colourful history of tribal communities is envisaged. Of course, on many occasions of our normal or day to day life we use some words which are nothing but abbreviated or aspirated types of the old ones just linked with the situation. In the local situational contexts many more so-called tribal communities have their placement in the normal setting and placed in such a situation, they have been reflected in popular usages, myths and mythological literature. In India, in course of time, Brahmin-dominated social systems made their way and thus some little compromise from time to time took place for depicting a social history of the situation. The name 'Santal' has its roots in 'Samanta Pal' i.e. border people as the local people used to call them. Actually, the Santals identify themselves as *hor* which means Man. *Ho, Horko,* etc. are associated with this term. Many foreign scholars used some terms which do not signify the original identity of the tribe.

We must not forget that Indian civilisation was founded not only by one group of people but by the combination of so many groups of people who came and interacted and, thus, in Indian civilisation we find the contribution of many groups - even of those who strayed far away from the ruling groups. While discussing the tribal history of this part of the country we have to accept and acknowledge the following groups and sub-groups who constituted it : the Santal, Kora, Kheria, Mahali, Birhor, Bhumij, Munda, Juang, Savar, etc. These are the autochthonese groups of people. In course of time they have been specially identified as separate groups, but in the truest sense, there are many more similarities on the basis of which we can reconstruct not only the tribal history but also the Indian history as a whole. However, we have to accept that many more so-called tribal words have been incorporated in the present Bengali language. Now, we are to depict the ethnographic details of the so-called tribal communities just to have the history of tribal India.

II

Santal : As it has been said that the Santals identify themselves as *hor* - meaning man. The total number of the Santals is about 40,00,000 (1991), though they are concentrated in Bihar, Orissa and Bengal and many of them are found in plantation areas as well as in encapsulated Bangladesh. The legendary genesis of the Santals is that once when the whole universe was full of water, two ducks were crying and out of their laying of two eggs the whole universe and human groups came into being and developed. These groups were basically agricultural communities in early times, they prefer to live near the jungles, clear patches of land and cultivate these for their livelihood. Sometimes, due to pressure on land some sections of them left for another area, specially the forest zones where they developed agriculture with subsidiary occupations like hunting and collecting games, roots and tubers. So they were conversant with the art of domestication of animals and as such in their houses they had the provisions for keeping many more domestic animals. Besides they had bows, arrows, spears and axes for hunting as well as for using as war weapons. In the villages, generally, they live together. Santal villages can be identified very clearly. There are lanes and bylanes; huts are arranged by the side of the road. There might be wells; in earlier times they used to take water from the ponds which they excavated for their own purpose. Santal huts are well-fenced-specially uncut bamboo branches are tied by means of bamboo slips and thus they appear thorny-fenced just to safeguard the domicile and protect the kitchen gardens so nicely prepared by both males and females. Throughout the year one can see the kitchen gardens full of many vegetables. A Santal village can be identified by watching the outer walls of the huts, which are beautifully decorated with coloured designs, sometimes with plain drawings of birds and leaves. The Santals bring a special type of clay for decorating purposes and thus reflect a sense of beauty and taste. Sometimes, a well-to-do Santal has a few huts–one for kitchen, another for sleeping and yet another to keep agricultural or hunting appliances. Even these domestic utensils are very neat and clean. One will be astonished to see on the head of a Santal woman a few earthen pots full of drinking water fetched from outside.

However, clear seasonal variations have a profound impact on their day-to-day life. In the villages, huts are arranged on both sides of the road. The place of the village tutelary deity is generally a banyan or *Mahul* tree where celebrations are held. In many cases, these trees are not available. Then a tree near the village dancing ground is selected for the annual village festival. Those who have a little commodious accommodation have a separate sleeping or working place. Otherwise poorer people have only one hut, in which cooking is done in one corner and agricultural appliances are kept, in another. Bows and arrows are hung separately along with clothes and other things. Now-a-days, the Santals keep one tin suitcase with lock and key arrangement to keep ornaments or money. In earlier times, bamboo baskets with lock and key arrangements were kept in the house. Aside from all these, the Santal hut is neat and clean and attracts the attention of other people.

They have all hunting appliances like bows, arrows, bolts and spears of different sizes. Though they are agriculturists, hunting is common to them and proves more attractive in their life. Except normal hunting there is a special hunting ceremony when they go to the Ayodhya hills of Purulia where all the Santals from different parts of this region assemble. This ceremony is generally held on the Bengali New-Year's Day. During the agricultural season they are extremely busy and do not spend a single minute in idleness. They work in their own homestead land or nearby villages as agricultural labourers. Now, after the establishment of the Left-Front ministry in this state, they get fixed labour charge per day.

Earlier, they were often cheated by the land holding communities. The Santals had to migrate to different parts of this state to work at different times. Sometimes as coolies on the railway platform, sometimes in preparing bricks, and sometimes again in expending manual labour for money in various areas of Kolkata and its vicinity, where daily wage earners are needed by the contractors.

In respect of social organisation family is the smallest unit. In most of the cases single unclear families are dominant. But sometimes we find joint or extended types of families. There is also evidence of polygyny. Generally male members are in a dominating position. Formal negotiations of marriage are started by the village *Manjhi* who has to negotiate with the parents of the prospective bride. In this way finalisation of the marriage date is made. Profuse rice bear is consumed in the family and in the neighbouring families.

They have an elaborate *panchayat* organisation having the following officials :

The Manjhi	-	Headman of the village. He represents the village in the relations with the outsiders.
The Paranik or Paramanik	-	The headman's assistant.

The Jog-manjhi	-	The master of ceremonies in dances, weddings, etc. He is also the moral censor of the village.
To Jog Paranick or Jog Paramanick	-	A deputy Jogmanjhi.
The Naikei	-	The village priest.
The Kudum Naikei	-	A deputy village priest. His duty is to ward off evil spirits by offering his own blood, obtained by scratching on his arm, and mixed with rice.
The Gorait or Kotal	-	The village messenger or peon.

However, there are a few reports where it is found that the Santals have got the benefit of the traditional panchayat in respect of the following :

> The holding of each *Rayats* has been accurately measured, defined and recorded in official papers at the time of settlement.

But, now-a-days, elected panchayats have to do this type of work. This is done in the party office before it is being executed and then this is communicated to the elected panchayat, not to the traditional panchayat.

It has been reported that before the Left-front rule in this state the following tenures are continued :

The Santals had the *Jamai* or *Jote* right. It was generally parmanent, temporary or verbal. The produce was to be divided in two, one half to be given to the cultivator and the others half to the owner.

But sometimes this right changed in *Tebhaga*. The cultivator had to cultivate the land and had to give only one third of this produce to the owner and two thirds including straw etc. would go to the cultivator. Now-a-days, this type of distribution of produce is resorted to when the owner of the land is a different man (other than the cultivator). The distribution was previously made by the village panchayat but now it is made by the elected panchayat. They are the final authority on production distribution. In complicated situations, Tribal Welfare Department Officers or elected panchayat members are urged to finalise the matter as the situation demands.

The village officials who have been mentioned early are generally selected in the village *Jaherthan* near the dancing place where the old big tree stands. In that place all formal elections take place. Dance performances and merry-makings at the time of any celebration of the village also take place there. Panchayat procedure is followed in the same place.

In the traditional village panchayat, headman is expected to participate in all important village affairs. In finalisation of disputes the headman's presence is needed. Even at the time of funeral rites and observations the headman is consulted.

However, the Manjhi is the village headman, his presence is needed in all affairs. He is the symbolic head of the village. He performs sacrificial rites at Manjhithan and in intervillage disputes, his presence is required. It has been said that *paranik* is an assistant to the headman. Sometimes his services are summoned by the village headman. Bodding (1935) describes the function of the Jogmanjhi as that of the guardian of morals. His most important function is to preside over the marriage ceremonies. At the Sohrai festival his function is very important as he has to guide one and all.

In respect of village organisation *Goret* has a definite role in working as a messenger to the headman. He takes news around the village, convenes the village people, collects funds on and for specific occasions and informs or alerts the villagers about any important event.

There are formal intervillage councils under the authority of *Parganait.*

Marriage, in Santal society, is considered a very significant event in domestic organisation. Among the Santals, illegitimacy never exists. The main restrictions on marriage are tribal endogamy, lineage endogamy, and exclusion of cross-cousins. The standard marriage form among the Santals is *Kirin Bahu Bapla,* contacted by families concerned through a middle man. But we find some instances of other forms of getting a mate in Santal society. These are also recognised by the society, but this should not violate exogamy rule or endogamy rule.

Bride price is paid by the groom's party in addition to the customary exchange of gifts. Expenditure to be incurred depends on the nature or type of marriage. This is treated all the time as a community affair. All these require involvement of the people or families as well as different degrees of social participation.

(1) *Tunki - Dipil - Bapla* is known as the regular form of marriage when brideprice is paid. Earlier it was less, but now-a-days it has been increased. Marriage is settled between two families through a middle man. In this form of marriage Jogmanjhi has to play a very important role. There are a series of rites and ceremonies and these are to be performed. There are songs and riddles in connection with the Santal marriage. Just to negotiate the marriage formalities, both the parties play

significant role. Of course, there are likings and dislikings on the part of the bride and the groom. They wait for proper indications which are known as *Sar Sagun*. These are carefully observed and on the basis of these marriage formalities continue. There are a few important events which are considered bad or good omens— if an individual with an axe or cutting implement, or a man with fire wood on his shoulder, or fire, snake or jackle is found on the way, then without the slightest hesitation the marriage proposal is thrown away or discarded. Sometimes, Jogmanjhi directs two or three girls to move along, bowing their heads and the bridegroom's party recognise the bride. This is done under the direction of the Jogmanjhi. Application of turmeric paste before the formal marriage is considered very important, Jogmanjhi, his wife, Naike, his wife, Manjhi and his wife of the respective villages go and anoint mustard oil and turmeric paste on body of the respective bride and the groom. Generally the bride groom goes to the house of the bride and they are to take one big open basket on their heads. At that time, the bride has to beat the prospective husband with fresh mango twigs. The bride all the while covers her face with the corner of her cloth. After a few minutes the groom removes the cloth from the face of the bride and applies vermilion on her forehead - then, the marriage ceremony is almost over, the bride is again anointed with vermilion paste by the brother of the groom. After that merry-making and dancing start and continue for about two days. Celebrations will be generally over after two days. During the time of marry-making, the bride goes back to her father's place.

(2) Another form of getting marriage is known as *Iputut* or marriage by force. If any man forcibly smears vermilion on the forehead of a mature girl, then the marriage is technically solemnised. Here, the bride may

have her slightest consent or may not have consent at all, but if vermilion is applied, the marriage is considered to be officially solemnised. But it is to be remembered that in *Iputut* marriage if the girl has no consent whatsoever, her family may go to the village council for settlement. Sometimes settlement is made when the groom offers a sumptuous feast to the neighbours of the girl. If the girl does not agree to the settlement, then formal divorce is sought and granted.

(3) *Apangir* is another form of marriage when a girl or even a married women is to cohabit with another man. Sometimes a girl is taken forcibly by the man and continues to live at his house as wife and husband. There was a custom that if any married women is forcibly taken away by a man and if he is caught, then severe torture was inflicted on him. The man might be killed mercilessly. In most of the cases the groom left the village with his wife. But very recently one case has been reported in Barageria, P.S. Narayangarh but due to the interference of the panchayat the man was not killed. The couple, however, left the village and went to a different place and now they are staying there as husband and wife.

Another type of marriage is performed by a poor man. As the bridegroom has not sufficient money for regular payment or other purposes he resorts to this type of marriage. The bride is brought to the house of the bridegroom with a small bamboo basket on her head. A few friends or relatives of the bride or the groom accompany her. The bridegroom, in presence of all the accompanying persons, applies vermilion mark on her forehead in order to solemnise the marriage. A feast is arranged according to the financial capacity of the groom and the couple begin to live as husband and wife.

(4) *Kudan Bapla* : If a girl becomes pregnant by a young man, she must marry him. The young man informs the Jogmanjhi about the situation and the girl has to confess to the wife of the Jogmanjhi. Then the Jogmanjhi informs the headman of the village and also the parents of the girls. Of course, the bridegroom has to pay a minimum sum of money Rs. 12. The Jogmanjhi then takes the couple to the house of the bridegroom and a date is fixed for formal marriage. On the fixed day, in the house of the bridegroom, vermilion mark is applied on the forehead of the bride. Then the marriage is formally accepted.

(5) *Kising Jawae* : If the couple belong to the same clan, the headman of the village calls the panchayat, and after some discussion, steps are generally taken accordingly. In this case, the boy's father has to bear the expenses of the marriage of the girl to another man. When the headman of the village arranges the marriage, provisions are made, so that the groom gets a cow and some money from the father of the guilty and the name is always kept a secret. As usual, the bride is to be offered to the groom, having been seated on a thin flat piece of wood, and the bridegroom applies vermilion on her forehead.

(6) *Gardi Jawae* : In this type of marriage the bridegroom has to stay as resident son-in-law because in the family there is only one daughter and no brother. There might be minor sons. Ghardi Jawae has to work with her wife's father in respect of agricultural activities. Or it might be that the girl is ugly in appearance, or deformed. Then the alternative is to bring a boy who will marry the daughter, and by virtue of the system he will enjoy the property of his father-in-law. Here is this type of marriage, the friends of the bride and the groom, take part. No official formalities are performed. As per

the custom the girl's father offers a calf to his resident son-in-law. If the man wants that the resident son-in-law be given anything, then that should be given. Of course, the daughter should be given separately from his belongings as well as from the property.

There is provision for divorce and the village council was to order and observe this provision. The parties concerned intimate this to the village council and according to their suggestions the Manjhis of both the villages, specially the elderly man, assemble together in a public place. Then the husband, in presence of the wife who is to be divorced, brings one *Sal* (Shorea robusta) leaf which is to be torn longitudinally straight. This is official divorce. Besides, one brass pot filled with water is to be turned by the groom simply by touching it with his feet. If water flows in the proper direction, then divorce is valid. If not, this type of marriage is against the customs. Hence killing or murder becomes unavoidable.

These are a few formalities in respect of the Santal marriage ceremony. Any sort of violation is seriously treated as it is the violation of the customary rules.

There are a few aspects of customs strictly to be followed by the Santals and these traditions are handed down to posterity. Any sort of shifting or deviation indicates violation of customary rules and for this community members, specially traditional village elders, have to take decisions and the mode of punishment which is generally traditionally fixed up is implemented. None of the community members are to violate the customs - as in the killing of the witches. In this way, the customary laws are being maintained, respected and obeyed by this group of people.

III

Mahali : Risley (1981), in his *Tribes and Castes of Bengal (Vol.II),* mentions the Mahalis but in his description many more complexities are noticed. He describes them as;

> Dravidian castes of labourers, palanquin bearers, and worker in bamboo, found in Chhotanagpur and western Bengal. They are divided into five sub-castes, branch of Santals, separate at a comparatively recent date from the parent tribe. The exact causes of separation are, of course, lost in the obscurity which enshrouds the early history of all the tribal movements. But the fact is that the Mahalis make baskets and carry palanquins, the occupations which every Santal would deem degrading, suggest that the adoption of these pursuit may have given the first impulse to the formation of a new group.

However, this report was prepared by Risley long ago and is now, practically, not valid. Recent work among these groups of people tells a different story.

Present researches disclose that the Mahalis were associated with the Santals and sometimes they were engaged as *Kheroal,* specially in times of battle with the outsiders. All these groups, i.e., the Santals and Mahalis have to work together during battle. It is said that the Mahalis provided the soldiers with 'Protectores; bows and shafts made of bamboo, were generally prepared by the Mahalis. This particular group of people gradually specialised in bamboo work and ultimately, as per the stipulations of the caste system, engaged mainly in bamboo work. In course of time, this became their parmanent profession. The name 'Mahali' originated from two words: 'Mah' which means bamboo and 'Ali' i.e., specialised. This is according to the legend which has been handed down to posterity. Even most of their clan names are similar to those of the Santals indicating that 'Santal' is the root. This section from the Santal imitated caste system specialised in bamboo work; hence they came to be known as Mahali.

They are patriarchate people. They have an elaborate clan organisation - clans are incidentally totemistic in nature. Somebody reported that 13 totemistic clans are present in the Mahali society. Marriage in the same clan is strictly prohibited. It is important to note that the clan names are closely related to the Santal clans. But there is also a little variation. Clan names are like (i) Besra, (ii) Hansda, (iii) Hembrom, (iv) Kisku, (v) Mandi, (vi) Baske, (vii) Murmu, (viii) Soren, (ix) Tudu, (x) Chore, (xi) Samah, (xii) Pirhi, (xiii) Khangar.

Of course, Risley referred to 34 clans among them. The clans have no discrimination. All the clans are equal in status. A few clans are again sub-grouped, like Mandi (totem : a kind of blue bird) locally known as *Nilchakra*. In the same way, Murmu has six sub groups. Again, Baske clans have three sub-divisions as in the case of Besra. Hemrom has three sub-divisions. In the same way Hansda has three sub-divisions. Tudu has two sub-divisions as in the case of Kisku. Soren clan has two sub-divisions. Chore clan has no sub-division such as in cases of Samah and Pirih and Khangar. These are not very common in the Mahali society.

In this connection it can be said that the Mahalis have five sub-groups:

(i) *Bansphor Mahali* - those who are basket-makers, i.e., bamboo workers.

(ii) *Pator Mahali or cultivators* - as well as basket-makers.

(iii) *Sulunki Mahali* i.e. cultivators and labourers.

(iv) *Tanti Mahali* - palanquin bearers.

(v) *Mahali-Munda* - their occupation not mentioned.

On local enquiry it is found that they admit 'Bansh Mahali' which might have been indicated by Risley as 'Bansphor Mahalis' (bamboo worker) - other sub-groups mentioned by Risley are not found in Midnapore.

However, there are many more indications that the Mahalis have originated from the big Santal or *hor* race. The Bedia group of people also assert themselves as 'Mahali'. Risley opined that the Mahali's rank might be equated with that of the Bauris. It is interesting to note, that like the Santals they also live in different parts of Bengal and this might be due to the compulsive' push' factor, i.e., just to have a comfortable way of life elsewhere.

The clans of the Mahalis adhere to their traditional norms, i.e., they are fully exogamous. They maintain a rigid stance of not marrying within the clan. And they are totemistic. Marriage within the clan is considered to be a punishable offence - a breach of customary laws. Through totemic origin the clan members are considered as brothers and sisters: so marriage within the same clan is strictly prohibited. Even emotional love within the same clan never happens. It is considered that emotional love or any sort of sexual offence within the same clan is strictly prohibited because there might be super-natural punishment.

It is found that some clans have minor privileges in their village life. Most of the village headmen are from the Mandi clan. The headman is known as the Manjhi. Next to the headman is the Gorait who is generally selected from the Basra clan. The deputy headman is known as the Paranik who in most cases is selected from the Baske clan. Yet it has been observed that the village priest or Naike and the ceremonial cook, i.e., Paranik belong to a particular family or to the Mandi and Baske clans respectively. Besides there is the Pargana who is generally elected from the Murmu clan and his main function is ceremonial immersion of the bones of the dead. Clan names are usually followed by the members of the descent. The fundamental obligation is that the Mahalis should bear the clan names as their surnames, excepting a few who have embraced Christianity. It is reported that in olden days they had to near different types of dresses but now-a-days these types are not prevalent.

It is also reported that specific types of clans have to face a particular direction at the time of worship, specially during a communal sacrifice. It is reported that the Murmu clan members face the east during a ceremonial sacrifice. The Sada Mandi sub-division does not use vermilion during worship and recites sacred formulae in a very low tone. The Mandi clan members use vermilion and recite sacred formulae in a loud tone and sacrifice white fowls. The members of the Murmu clan first sacrifice a red fowl in the same way the Baske clan members sacrifice a mixed coloured (Baranunia) fowl to their Orak Bonga (family deity). Members of the Besra clan sacrifice a red cock for propitiation of some deities. While offering this sacrifice, he sits with folded knees. Members of the Tudu clan lift their offerings before the deities and often they sit with folded knees, touching the ground, while the members of Kisku clan offer the articles with folded knees, touching their breast to the ground. Thus, it is clear that almost all the clans have to follow a traditional system of offering sacrifices even today, and these have not yet been changed though some of the members have received higher education.

Again, disposal of the dead is a specific type of ritual and this has been followed generation after generation.

For this ritual no scientific explanations are offered. It is observed that at the time of burial or cremation, the head of the dead is kept towards north except among the Mandis and Murmus who place the head of the dead towards east. Naturally, the traditional pattern is still observed and this continues as per customs.

In the same way, birth ritual, ceremonial name giving, purification ceremony after birth, do not differ from clan to clan.

> Only the case of *sada* sub-division of Mandi, Murmu Baske, Hemrom and Kisku do not use clothes anointed with turmeric during marriage. They prefer to use white cloth. In the same way Sak sub-division of Hansda, Soren clan members do not use conch-shell and white necklace of coatries during marriage.
>
> (Sengupta : 32)

But as in most of the tribal clans, the observances are supplemented by special food taboos as these are considered very important.

There are different types of food taboos; some food is forbidden to a particular type of clan. The Mandi clan does not consume pineapple.

There are many more restrictions which are handed down to posterity. Members of different clans do not consume green mango unless the *Baha,* first flower blooming festival is held. Such is the case of using *Mahua* (Madhuka Latifolia) flowers, even new paddy, until they perform the first fruit-eating ceremony, offering fruit to the deities.

There are a few formal prohibitions or taboos at the time of pregnancy. The pregnant women never observe food taboos but there are other prohibitions specially on going to some places.

Some unholy places like the cremation ground should not be visited by a pregnant women; this is because some ghosts or spirits are believed reside in those places and they may catch hold the pregnant woman, which may cause danger to the baby in the womb. Distant travels are also prohibited; generally a male member accompanies her to a distant place. Fishes caught in a basket trap or in hook are forbidden for consumption. The idea behind this is that there might be difficulties at the time of delivery, causing lingering pain. The pregnant women are advised not to sew torn pieces of cloth with needle; this may cause blindness to the newborn baby. Preparation of cakes is prohibited with the belief that the baby may be of cleft-lip. Jackfruit, wood apple or pineapple-eating is strictly prohibited.

On the 10th day after birth a purificatory ceremony is performed - the room is sprinkled with fresh water - the mother is allowed to cook or engage in a little bit of physical labour. On the 21st day after the birth of a child a ceremonial feast is arranged for some members of the community. The barber has to pare off the nails of the mother and the child. At the time, the name giving ceremony is held. A barber attends the ceremony. A feast is expected to be given to the relatives as per those economic condition of the family.

In respect of marriage, there are certain prohibitions—marriage in the same clan groups and immediate kin groups is prohibited. Again, blood kins and close classificatory relations, even children of the ritual kins, are not all permitted for marriage. Bride-price is common; a man spends money for his daughter, but it is customary that the bride-price is paid ceremonially to the tune of Rs. 24. Three pieces of cloth, one for the bride's mother, one for the foster mother or *dai* and one for the bride, are to be given. Marriage by intrusion also takes place when the prospective bride forcibly enters the house of the man whom she likes. This is locally known as the *Ghor meehrane.* Of course, ill treatment follows, but, in spite of this, if she wants to continue the relationship there, ultimately there will be a parmanent union having social approval. Marriage by elopment is not very common but it is approved and formally known as *amapar,* Tana or 'pulling' - when a man forcibly takes the girl and puts on her forehead vermilion mark. Ultimately these marriages are reported to the village council and after sometime these are approved. Before the finalisation of marriage, bride-price is paid. Widow remarriage or *Sanga* is prevalent, but the opinion of the village elders is needed. Marriage by mutual consent also prevails.

However, before the finalisation of marriage there are a few formal ceremonies. Bride price is fixed and this is to be paid. Sometimes it is Rs. 15. This is the custom —until it is not paid, the marriage is not considered valid. As per the formal procedure the elderly people of the bride's village come for finalising the marriage date. The Manjhi of the bridegroom's village must be present at the time of the formal payment of bride price. Then the bridegroom's party come ceremonically to the bride's village with their village Manjhi. They are cordially received. On that day Manjhis of bride's village along with a few elderly person receive the wedding party cordially. The bridegroom, in presence of the assembled parties, applies the vermilion mark on the forehead and hairparting of the bride. An iron bangle is made to cover the right wrist of the bride and after this the bridegroom declares that the girl will be treated as his wife.

After death, cremation is the custom. Females are prohibited to go the cremation ground. Some minor rituals are performed at the cremation ground. Burnt charcoal from the pyre is kept in an earthen pot and this is placed on the main road on the day of the *Sudh* (purificatory) ceremony. The Paranik has to cook and the foods is placed on a *sal* leaf and then kept on the street. Then other formalities are continued victims of small-pox are generally buried, but this disease is now non-existent.

Though there are formally elected gram sabha and panchayat in which elected members have to function, there is the traditional village panchayat consisting of senior members of the community. In a few cases it is found that some more villagers of different castes and communities take part and give their opinions for setling dispute, though they do not belong to the Mahali tribe. Issue of disputes are discussed and afterwards decision is taken. The traditional village council or sabha is constituted with the following village officials:

(i) *Manjhi Haram* - Headman.

(ii) *Gorait* - Village messenger as well as assistant to Manjhi Haram.

(iii) *Paranik* - Deputy headman.

The post of the Manjhi Haram is hereditary. Generally, he belongs to the Mandi clan. The headman is practically nominated by him. It is preferable that the youngest son should be nominated. Of course, the village elders help him in finalising the selection. Both the Gorait and the Paranik place suggestions in finalising the selection. The post of the Gorait is hereditary; so is the next post of the village official, i.e., Paranik.

In this connection it can be said that the village officials receive special honour. During marriage celebrations the headman gets a special royalty i.e., ten betel leaves and ten nuts, sometimes a piece of new cloth during the solemnisation of marriage, sometimes a token cash amount is also offered to him. Marriage negotiations are also finalised in his presence, formal bride-price is also paid. During worships, not only subscriptions are collected in his presence but also articles are purchased under his total supervision. In the same way the Gorait has also to perform certain duties in connection with marriage and other village festivals. In case of a second marriage, the Gorait is informed first. The Paranik has to be involved in all these matters as per customs.

Cases like adultery, illicit love, witchcraft, practice of black magic, breach of traditional taboos, defiance of the order of the village council, are generally considered as offences which the village council has to deal with. However, it is to be noted carefully that all matter of village problems arising out of interaction should be finalised by the non-traditional panchayat members.

It has been reported that at present, the affairs related to the community are discussed by the tribal council; the elected body of the present panchayat is never asked to discuss them because in the elected Panchayat many other persons are there including the non-Mahalis. So only their own problems get the topmost priority. But there are a few cases when the traditional village council members fail to take any decision and refer them to the elected *Gram Sabha* whose verdict is final.

Another important matter is now surfacing. A section of the Mahalis along with the other tribal groups are having support as members of the Jharkhand party who want a separate state. Here also we find other groups of people both tribals and non-tribals who want to support Jharkhand interact together. At the sametime, the Mahalis, backed by their sentiments and emotions have gradually, formed an organisation, named 'Paschim Banga Mahali Samaj Kalyan Samiti' and thus an ingroup mentality is going to be crystallised. That may encourage to inculcate many more traditional customs which are in a fading state.

IV

Kora : The Koras are also one of little known tribes in West Bengal though they are distributed in many districts, specially Midnapur, Burdwan and Bankura. Risley (1891) seems to be confused when he describes them thus :

> A Dravidian caste of earth ,workers and cultivators in Chotanagpur, western and central Bengal probably an offshoot from a Munda tribe. The Koras or Khayras of Manbhum and Bankura have well marked totemistic societies of the same tribe as the Mundas, and the later admit that some sort of affinity may at one time have been recognised .... They have a curious legend concerning their totem.

However, recent researches have thrown new light on the origin and development of the tribe. In West Bengal, they are treated as one of the Scheduled tribes entitled to have constitutional benefits.

The Koras are one of the 'Austro-Asiatic' speaking tribes. It is generally believed that 'Kora' - means 'small'. May be this group of Austro-Asiatic speaking is considered to be small or lower in socio-economic status and hence it is termed 'Kora' when compared with the Santal. It has been observed that this group of people engage in digging or rather earth work which the Santal and others regard as 'low-status occupation'. The major economic roles played by the Kora concern their occupations as agricultural labourers rather earth cutters, i.e., digging tanks, doing construction work and repairing of roads. This sort of poor and unpredictable economy puts the people in difficulties and as a result their socio-economic status is low. Of course, Grierson states that the Koras use the surname 'Modi' and that their language is derived from Mundari. Regarding their dialect it can be said that they are well versed in local Bengali, though their women are not so much fluent in the language.

Apropos of their occupations they are very capable of digging and as such earth work in considered almost their main occupation. But in reality they are an agricultural group of people having an improverished economy. In the truest sense a good many Koras have land of just a few bighas and as such agriculture may be considered their main occupation. Their huts are small—with mudbuilt walls and covered with straw. There are courtyard and extra land in and around each hut. Sometimes the land is not fully cultivated, but kept barren. However, the substantive economy of the Koras is agriculture. It is interesting to note that a few festivals are associated with their agricultural activities, like the application of vermilion marks on the bullock, the plough share, etc. indicating religiosity which is however not insistent on the employment of any Brahmin priests. There is also the *Jathel* festival before harvesting in front of the tutelary village deity. Their dress is like a local peasant's dress, *dhoti* for the male and *sari* for the female, but children or those who have a little education or earning capacity are found to use trousers, *payjama* and shirt.

They have clans with respective totems. Marriage within the clan is strictly prohibited and clans are totemic in nature. Each clan has a name derived from a plant, fruit or an animal. The clan members never intermarry. A few clans are as follows : *Samcr* (Sal fish), *Hara* (Turtle), *Memrom* (Arcanut), *Sapu* (Kite), *Lodham* (Squirrel), *Bhutku* (Pig), *Barda* (a kind of tree), *Hansda* (Wild goose), *Kasibak* (Heron), *Balishay* (Tortoise), etc.

Their family is small in size, having a nucleus consisting of parents and unmarried children. In respect of kinship the Koras have both classificatory and descriptive types of kin. But it is important to note that the 'Kinship' term is like that of local Bengali people. In respect of the life cycle procedure, the commencement of pregnancy is simply recorded and intimated to the elderly members of the family. Of course, certain precautionery measures are taken to avoid illness. Delivery takes place in the dwelling-house of the owner. The delivery room is in one corner of the small hut. Some elderly female members are asked to help in the delivery cases. It is to note that only female members are allowed to enter the delivery room. The period of pollution continues for nine days, but in some cases it continues upto 21 days. This pollution period is applicable only to the family members. Nobody can take part in any religious activities of the village. Of course, the day of purification is fixed when the formal name giving ceremony is held. The local barber is asked to take part in it. He/she is engaged in ceremonial name giving formalities and pares off the nails of the new born child. The mother and the child are given ceremonial bath; the entire house is washed with cowdung solution. Old clothes are washed and changed and leaves of *Tulasi* are sunk in water and then sprinkled in the room as part of the purificatory ceremony. After that the newborn child is brought to the courtyard and is placed on a mat on which a piece of folded torn cloth is spread out. One of the elderly women puts a cup of water, three grains of rice, the first representing the supreme deity, as witness of the ceremony, the second representing one of the ancestors of the child. The name proposed to be given is uttered by any elderly man and if the floating grains meet together then it is believed that the ancestors are pleased to accept the name. If any difficulties arise then the procedure is repeated till all grains touch each other. The child is blessed by the members participating in this ceremony. Generally a feast is given for the assembled guests on the occasion. First, the rice-eating ceremony (Bhujna) takes place when the child becomes six or seven months old. This is finalised after consulting the almanac. Porridge or *payesh* is prepared out of milk, sweets - the elderly persons have to bless the child. If possible, some little sweet is presented to all the invitees. The child is gradually acquainted with toilet training sometimes small pieces of cloth or pants are given. The child can sleep with the mother upto the age of 5 - 6, until a new child is born. If not, he/she is given a special sleeping place preferably with the father or other senior members, or elderly brother and sister.

Among the Koras, monogamy is preferred, but polygyny, i.e., marriage with many women is very rare. Again, marriage takes place when the girl attains puberty. Risley says : (1969)

> The Koras of West Bengal marry their daughters both as infants and as adults. In Bengal the caste has fully adopted the more fashionable custom of marriage.

The marriage arrangements are generally made by the parents of the bride and the bridegroom and their kinsmen. There might be a go-between (Agna) just to facilitate marriage ceremony. No cross-cousin or parallel-cousin marriage is preferable. However, marriage is held by a token payment of bride price which is Rs. 12.50. It must be paid before the finalisation of marriage; otherwise the bridegroom will never take food in the house of his father-in-law. There are some other formalities like fixation of the date. Specially the Bengali almanac is followed by them. As per the customs of the local Bengali caste groups they avoid *Chaitra* (March-April), *Bhadra* (August-September), *Jaistha* (May-June), *Asarh* (June-July), *Sravan* (July-August). Besides, the birth-months of the bride and the groom are strictly prohibited in the choice of the dates for marriage. Like the members of the local Hindu caste, they consult the almanac as well as the local Brahmans who generally give their opinion.

There are some other formalities. Before the wedding date is finalised both the bridegroom and the bride are to follow certain formalities, like anointment of turmeric paste atleast for three consecutive days.

Marriage takes place in the house of the bride. It indicates that the bridegroom has to come to the bride's house. On that occasion the wife of the village *Manjhi* has to wash the feet of the groom's party. It is formal and there is no alternative. Practically the Manjhi is known as the Manjhi Haram. On that day a formal propitiation ceremony takes place; it is popularly known as *Chhamra Puja* celebrated for the welfare of the bridegroom. Two new earthen pitchers are filled by water by the headman and these are ceremonially placed in a corner of the marriage booth. Mango twigs are kept in the mouth of the earthen pitcher. Some quantity of pulses (Biri) are ceremonially kept inside the earthen pitcher. This is meant to pray to the supreme deity for the prosperity of the bridegroom and his party who are to proceed for the wedding purposes. In the same way the bride's house is decorated. All the formalities are observed there, as they are in the house of the bridegroom.

It is one of the formalities that the bridegroom's party will take with them three pieces of cloth, one for the bride's mother, one for the bride's father and the remaining one for the bride's brother.

When the bridegroom's party reaches the bride's village they are received by the bride's party and are accommodated for the night in a separate room.

Next, the bridegroom is brought to the marriage booth when a ceremony known as *Chuman* (kissing or welcoming) is performed. A brass plate with lighted earthen lamps on it is waved in front of bridegroom specially to his face by the bride's brother's wife or any other elderly married woman of the bride's family. This is the official reception. After that the bride is carried to the lap of the groom's elder brother's wife and then to the *Chhamra* (booth) three times. In a similar way, the groom is carried on the lap of the sister's husband and taken round three times. After that both the bride and the groom are asked to stand face to face when the groom applies vermilion mark on the forehead and the hair parting of the bride three times. The bride also puts vermilion mark on the forehead of the groom. This solemnizes the marriage formalities.

Of course, Risley (Reprint: 1969) remarks in a different way on the marriage ceremony of the Koras of Bankura, He says that it differs from that of the Singhbhum Koras. There the bride and the groom are allowed to stand on a bundle of straw. In the evening the bridegroom's party return to the village with the bride and are cordially received by the groom's mother as well as by other elderly female members. On the eighth day after marriage the groom visits his in-law's house; this is known as *Atmangala* i.e., the 'auspicious eighth' day. A new piece of cloth or *dhuti* is presented on this occasion by the bride's father to the groom. After staying for two days in the father-in-law's house, the couple return to their own house now. It is observed that, the sister's husband plays an important role in tying yellow-dyed threads on the wrists of the two - i.e., the couple.

Widow remarriage is permitted and is known as *Sangai*. In this case no bride price is paid; at the same time, there is no application of vermilion mark on the forehead of the women. In such marriage, the deceased husband's elder brother is never married, but the younger brother has the requisite permission. It is important to note here that the *Sangai* husband does not put vermilion mark on the forehead of the widow, but vermilion is smeared on her face generally by some other widows.

Divorce is granted by the village council.

It has been observed that a Kora boy of Banpatna Khelar, became involved in love with a Santal girl of the same village. The village elders became angry as this was not considered customary. Naturally, the head of that village intimated to the elders of neighbouring ten villages who participated in a discussion and came to the conclusion that the boy must apologise before the ten heads and entertain them. This would lead to the confirmation of the deviant situation, which was not formal.

After pregnancy they observe many rituals. Even after delivery the placenta is buried in the kitchen, specially in the south-eastern corner of the house.

In respect of death, cremation is considered to be formal when the head of the deadman is placed towards north. For carrying the dead to the cremation ground a bier is prepared out of bamboo and while carrying the dead they shout in the name of Hari, indicating the normal Hindu method of cremation. The eldest son generally applies the fire first to the mouth of the dead man's face kept towards the ground.

They also take bath after the cremation and with the leaves of *Tulasi* they purify themselves. Cremation is all the time preferable on any occasion of death. Purificatory ceremony is held on the 11th day. One barber is asked to shave the head or moustache and to pare off the nails. Before the ceremonial bath, mustard oil and turmeric paste are rubbed on the bodies of all the persons who participated in the funeral ceremony or the members of the bereaved. Assistance of low-status Brahmin is made available. It is to be noted that, at the place of cremation, a miniature mudbuilt body is prepared where the pyre was built. Again, a miniature hut of straw is prepared by the son of the departed. Fire is applied to it and then the son of the departed shouts: 'Your hut is being burnt. You come back to your own house.' It is nothing but the calling back of the departed soul.

In some cases it is reported that in many cases the Koras dispose their dead. When their heads are kept towards north.

In respect of inheritance of property male line is preferred. A daughter generally does not get any share.

Regarding the social position of the Koras, Risley notes:

> The social position of the Koras is very low and they are usually classed with the Bagdis, Bauris, Buras and other dwellers on the confined of Hinduism.
>
> (Vol. I, p. 510)

In village organisation the head of the *Panch* is known as the *Manjhi*. If marriage takes place in the same village with another caste or community member then the village panchayat sitting together makes a compromise and accepts the couple in the society. At the same time the panchayat plays a very important role in conflicting situations. In most of the cases elderly persons sit together and try to come to a concrete conclusion by which discipline is maintained.

The Koras have three important festivals. One is the Maghi puja. It is generally held on the last day of *Paush* (Jan-Feb). On that day, in the village public place, one fowl is sacrificed by the village priest. Again, on the last day of the Bengali year i.e., *Chaitra Sankantri* (15 April) one red cock is sacrified to appease the hovering spirits. This is known as the *Salai* festival when, in the world of nature, flowers blossom and new leaves come up. Another important festival popularly known as *Asharipuja* or Janthelpuja performed by the villagers. The date is not a fixed one, but it should be either a Tuesday or a Saturday. Here only the caste groups participate. They dance and sing songs just to forest much of their humdrum drudgery.

However, the Koras, one of the Austric-speaking tribes, gradually transformed into a type of the local caste group, but still many customs prevail and dominate among them to make them stand on a common platform to have a common tribal identity.

IV

Kharia : The earliest account of the Kharia was given by Col. Dalton (1866) in the *Journal of Asiatic Society*. In 1868 Ball described the 'Kharias of Dhalbhum', T.C. Das, S.C. Ray and R.C. Ray gave a detailed account of the Kharias. There are many more references to the Kharias. T.C. Das described the Kharias of Dhalbhum in the form of ethnography. Sometimes the Kharias were bracketed together or amalgamated with the Lodhas or the Savars, but this admixture is not justified.

It is true that they live in small villages situated in inaccessible forest tracts inextricably bound up with the vast world of nature. Their adaptation to the environment is direct and simple. Their level of technology is just enough to cope with their gathering economy. It is true that most of them lead of 'natural man' in the blissful environment enjoying the bounties of nature; they consider themselves as the masters of the forest tracts they inhabit and as such many clan names become associated with the territory concerned. It can be said that their forest habitats sustained them as there was less pressure on forests and forest management rules were liberal. With the development of the forest policy and rise of commercial forestry restrictions on the use of forests including collection of forest produce have been progressively brought into force. The Kharias are sub-divided into three distinct divisions; Pahari or Erenga Kharia, Dhelki Kharia and Dudh Kharia. It is said that their main habitation is Mayurbhanj in Orissa. Of course, due to historical upheavals, they have come in touch with the tribal groups of the locality. Some of the Hill Kharias consider themselves as Savars. As a result, the tradition introduced by the ancestors of the Hill Kharias is known as Sabhar-Buri. Many of the Kharias affiliate themselves with the mythological leader Jara Savar and many others put them into the Munda group. The Dhelki Kharias recount that the home of their descendants was Rohtasgarh. Some said that they had sprung from the society where they were driven from the country and then they came to the valley of Koel. Their relation with the Mundas was fraternal.

The material handled here relates to the Kharias of West Bengal and as such they have been categorised as Hill Kharia or Erenga Kharia. However, they have many clans. These are (1) Galgu (salfish), (2) Bhuiya (fish), (3)

Jaru (rat), (4) Budya (tuber), (5) Tesa (bird), (6) Hemrom (betel nut), (7) Bhuya Tensa (kind of bird), (8) Sal Bhuiya (sal fruit), (9) Tiring Bhula (a kind of bird), (10) Pichla Buta, (11) Dharbhula, (12) Bhujamarch (a kind of small fish), (13) Dharam Bandha Kawri (dog), (14) Alkusha (a kind of fruit), (15) Dondra (leaf cup), (16) Khela Kamar, (17) Gorai Mach (one type of fish), (18) Kurkut (a kind of red ant), (19) Pecha Gulgu (one type of bird).

As regards the customs is connection with birth, they observe a period of pollution. They believe that the successful birth of a child depends on the grace of the spirits. Sometimes malevolent spirits locally known as *Panchna Bhut* cause the death of a child either in the womb or after the birth. It may be noted that stoppage of menstruation is first considered as the symptom of conception. Then they observe certain taboos. These are: they should not eat rat, or *Dhemna* snake, they should visit the huts of men whose family members died recently, they should not cross a stream or drain, they should not eat fish caught by a trap, net or rod and line, they should not wear new clothes or buy new pots from the potter's hut.

In connection with birth it is to be remembered that the umbilical cord is cut by means of an arrow head - by any elderly women of the village. A little quantity of paddy is given to her as her honorarium. The placenta is buried near the hearth. Of course, the pollution period varies from three, five, seven to nine days. For this some more formalities are performed as per customs and these are all compulsory. After seven or nine days the pollution period is over and then one fowl is sacrificed. The lineage members or the members of the village take bath in a nearby pond. It is reported that on that day a feast is given. After five days, the head of the child is shaven. Earthen cooking utensils are thrown away and the family arranges a feast. The local Hindi word *Biha* is used for marriage. It takes place when girls attain the age of puberty. Preliminiary negotiations start with the parents of the bridegroom. Parents have to search for a suitable girl. There is one go between *(Raibyasha)* who helps the bridegroom's party visit the bride's place just to have a formal consent. Negotiations are usually conducted in a humorous way. The following may serve as an instance of characteristic humour:

> So many decades have elapsed but we have not seen so many people coming together.

The groom's party answer :

> One bird has been causing a great deal of destruction in our hamlet, killing fowl, spoiling *bajra* and *maize*, etc.

After some exchange of bantering words the bridegroom's party will ask for the price of the bride. The transanction occurs through the middleman. The bridegroom's party will take out a few maize seeds and place ten seeds as their price. Then these are transferred three times, i.e., by giving and returning; the number of seeds increases to 50 and the bridegroom's party will ask whether the bride's people are satisfied. They will answer in the negative. However, now-a-days the bride price varies from Rs. 20 to Rs. 50. Then the bride's party place a small quantity of rice and mustard oil on a *Sal* leaf plate and generally request the groom's party to take them. In this way negotiations continue. There is a custom that the groom has to undergo a test of ability to demonstrate whether he is capable of looking after his wife by taking the would be bride with him. Indeed, they move to the jungle, accompanied by a few relatives from each side to the jungle. There a big tree with a honey comb in it is selected. The prospective bridegroom will climb the tree carrying along the bride and some instruments to break the honey comb. If he becomes successful, then the marriage takes place.

However, at present, the procedure of the selection of bride has become less elaborate. The bridegroom's party does not consist of more than two persons; this may be due to economic stringency. Now-a-days, the formal ceremony of showing the efficiency of the bridegroom does not exist at all; specially in West Bengal Kharia villages the bridegroom's party with the maternal uncle come to the bride's village and they are allowed to stay a little distance away from the bride's hut. A shed is prepared and there a deity (Murmu) is placed. The *Chhamra* or *cover* is prepared by the leaves, specially of *Sal* or *Mahua*. It is interesting to note that two branches, one is *Mohua* and the other is *Sidha,* are planted by its side. Two earthen pots carried by the bride's grandmother or a woman akin to the grand. mother in relation are taken to the booth. The women demand some *paisa*. They sing marriage songs. Near the pool where water is to be taken, two pots are worshipped by application of vermilion and sundried rice. Of course, one pot must be carried by the grand. mother, another pot by any woman of the village. After bringing the pots, they demand some *paisa* from the parents of the bride. They are presented with a little amount of flattened rice or molasses at that time. There are other formalities: the brother-in-law has to dig up a long furrow towards the east-west direction. On the right hand side of the furrow, a banana plant is placed, while on the left hand side an arrow is placed. Three small wooden planks are then placed horizontally to the furrow.

In the evening the groom's party is expected to arrive. It is to be noted that the bride is ceremonially allowed to sit on a brass pot which is carried to the marriage booth by a few persons of the groom's party. She is then made to sit by the side of marriage booth *(Marua)* facing east. The groom is carried by his maternal uncle and is made to encircle the bride three times, facing west. After the formalities, the presiding deity of the *Marua*, the *Dharam*, i.e., the god of righteousness and *Kandhni randhni*, the presiding deity of children, are worshipped. The bride is taken to a natural pool by the maternal uncle for bathing. After her bath, she is brought to the *Marua* where she embraces the banana plant three times. She is then allowed to sit on a palm-leaf mat. Another interesting ritual is performed. The brother-in-law *(Bahani)* of the bride encircles seven strands of thread around the little toe of the bride's left leg and her left ear. Then a betel nut and a bangle of iron are tied to the threads. This is a must to solemnise the marriage of the Hill Kharias. The bride's body is anointed with mustard oil and turmeric paste. After these formalities, the bride's brother-in-law or grandfather slips the sacred thread on the neck of the bride and the bangle to her right fore-arm. Then the brother-in-law takes out some hair of the forehead and twists them into a lock. Out of this fore lock, two are dropped in the turmeric mixed oil which is made to drop down to her left leg. The third drop of oil is applied on her head. After this is over, the brother-in-law carries the bride inside the hut. The groom's party is again seen to carry her back to the *Marua* where she is given a leaf smeared with vermilion and oil. The groom snatches this off from her hand and keeps it by his side. He then removes the veil of the bride and vermilion is applied on the forehead of the bride. After this formal ceremony both the groom and the bride stand facing each other and sprinkle water on each other with mango twigs from the pot kept there earlier.

After this formality, the groom's party takes the bride and the groom inside a hut. The younger sisters of the bride wash the feet of the couple. For this they are given a token payment.

The bride and the groom are entertained with flattened rice and molasses separately. It is interesting to note that the groom formally refuses to take food but when the father-in-law promises to give something as presentation, he agrees. The promise is of all sorts of comforts, but now-a-days only a new cloth is given.

Next day one *Sal* leaf is smeared with vermilion and kept on the sacred *Tulasi Pira*. Then all the villagers are formally invited to touch the leaf. After that, people from the bride's house request the groom's party to have food.

Next day, the newly-married couple leave for the groom's village. Before the couple depart there are a few formalities to be observed. The bride is made to sit on a wooden plank. The father of the bride pours a little quantity of rice on the corner of her cloth. She is ceremonially asked by her mother: "My darling, where are you going?" She replies smilingly: 'I am going to work'. Then the rice is thrown and collected by the groom's party. It is nothing but a supernatural sanction. The ceremony has been minutely observed by Sinha (1984:34).

> The after marriage is over and when the bride and the groom start for the village of the groom, both of them are made to stand facing each other. The bride's hand is placed in the groom's hand, both their palms facing upward and fingers spread apart. The fathers of the bride and the groom bring out two arrow shafts and pass them through the gap of middle and fourth fingers of the bride and the groom from below. Then the two arrows are exchanged, after this the supernatural deity is

> invoked to witness the union and if the match is not lawful, the deity is enjoined to show the disapproval by breaking a tree's branch.

Marriage between the cross cousins or within blood relations is strictly prohibited; so is marriage with agnatic kins. There was a firm belief that marriage with other tribes or castes was a social crime and that the persons were to be expelled from the society. As the group of people are patrilocal, girls go to live in their husbands, place after marriage. When the bride has no brother, the groom may go to stay in the house of his wife's father. Marriage by elopement or intrusion, marriage by forcible application of vermilion, and love marriage are all considered to be within the same category as elopement. Sorrorate, levirate, widow remarriage is sanctioned under certain conditions.

V

Munda : The Mundas are one of the 'Kolian'* groups of people inhabiting mainly the Chotanagpur plateau. The Ranchi district in Bihar state is the principal home of the Mundas, they generally occupy the southern, south-western and eastern parts of this district. Now they are found to have migrated to the adjoining states. In West Bengal especially their number is not insignificant.

---

*Most of the early writers described the Mundas as 'Kolarians'. Dalton classifies them as Kolarians along with the Hos, Bhumijes, Juangs, Kharias, Santals, Birhors, Morwas, Kurs and Kurkus or Muasis. Risley (1872) describes the Mundas as them Kolarian group of people. S.C. Roy (1912) considers them as members of the so-called Kolarian tribes inhabiting the Chotanagpur division (p. 355). Now, the question is point if they are treated as a 'Kol' group of people, they should rightly be called 'Kolian'. Prof. S.K. Chatterjee (1923) objects to the use of the term 'Kolarian' to identify the Mundari group of people.

The name "Munda" is of Sanskrit origion,

> "It means the headman of a village, and is a tutelary or functional designation used by the members of the tribe, as well as by outsiders".

The Mundas call themselves 'Horo-Ko' (man or human being), Roy traces their original home to a distant "land of eighty-one uplands and eighty-three elevated rice fields" - a celebrated tradition handed down to posterity in the Mundari legend (Roy 1912 : 10). Besides, the name of their traditional god 'Marang Buru' connotes a 'great mountain', and this indicates their possible homeland.

The Mundas are good agriculturists and they cultivate lands, where they settled. Their wanderings and migrations at later stages were possibly due to their search for good cultivable lands and better occupations and, at the same time, to the pressure exerted on them by one of their more vigorous neighbouring communities, the Oraons. Sometimes during such migrations, they settled in West Bengal which fringes the Ranchi plateau. Three distinct zones of their migration in West Bengal can be categorised on the basis of ecological differences:

(1) the west Midnapur region, which is an extension of the Chotanagpur plateau, where migration was easy and spontaneous; (2) the region of lower Bengal, specially 24-Parganas, where they came early as indigo-plantation labourers, and later were recruited as "hewers of wood and drawers of water" in the jungles of the Sunderbans; and (3) the North Bengal region, where they were recruited as plantation labourers. They came there in successive waves and later on cleared some regions round about the tea estates forming satellite villages. They engaged in some casual labour at plantations and supplemented their income by agriculture.

It has been attempted to know how far their customary laws are operating in the present context. As such only three districts of the frontier tract have been chosen for intensive study.

The Mundas are a patrilineal tribe. Risley (1969) observes thirteen sub-tribes among them. These are, according to him, (1) Kharia-Munda, (2) Karanga-Munda, (3) Kol-Munda, (4) Mahali-Munda, (5) Oraon-Munda, (6) Savar-Munda - possibly crossing with the neighbouring tribes, (7) Bhuinhar-Munda, (8) Manki-Munda, (9) Khangar-Munda, (10) Kongput-Munda, (11) Nagbanshi-Munda, (12) Munda-Manjhi and (13) Sad-Munda, so named possibly due to the association of the tribe with a particular locality or status like most of the tribal people of India, the Mundas are divided into a number of clans or *Kilis*. Risley gives a long list of the *Kilis*. The members of the *Kilis* associate themselves with some particular totems, which are either plants, animals or natural bodies. There are many stories regarding the origin of these totems and their association with such groups. S.C. Roy refers to 36 clans and accepts the gradual sub-division of the clans as they dispersed into different tracts of the country. He narrates a number of stories relating to the gradual changes in the names of the clans as well as in the division of the clans. He further observes :

> This sub-division was probably effected to avoid the necessity of the members of one *Kili* having to travel a long way off into the domain of another *Kili* to seek wives for their sons or husbands of their daughters.
>
> (*op. cit.*, 405)

Though the origin of the *Kilis* or *Gotra*-names is fabulous and unrealistic, one can easily realize the inter-connection of the members of the *Gotra* with that of the totem. Generally, a clan meant a consanguinous kinship either genealogically or fictionally definable. This is applicable to the Mundas of other districts except those of Midnapur. However, a few interesting stories regarding the origin of the clan are given here to show its unrealistic connection with the totems and the clan members. Regarding the origin of the Kachhim (*Kachchua* or tortoise) clan there is a story prevalent, which slightly differs from that in the account of Roy. Once, due to a sudden flood, a number of men and other animals were carried away by strong currents. The flood was so intense that everybody was frantically striving to get on to a piece of hard soil somehow or other. At that time a man saw a tortoise near a bush of reeds. He got afraid and gradually lost his sense. At the same time the tortoise also got afraid. Then, all on a sudden, the tortoise dipped into the water and disappeared and crawled on to the other side of the river in spate. There he found another man coming to him. Out of fear the tortoise again dipped and came to the place where the unconscious man remained floating on the water. The man who tried to catch the tortoise followed it and suddenly found that another man was floating there. Then he took the man out of water, nursed him and gradually brought him back to consciousness. Then he understood that it was because of the tortoise that he had been saved by a fellow-man and from that time on he considered the tortoise as his saviour and all his family members started paying respect to it regularly. The tortoise is considered by the members of that family as the incarnation of a god.

The members of each clan observe certain restrictions in respect of a totem. They do not kill, injure or even touch their respective totemic objects. Violation of such taboos is considered a serious sin by the clan members. All the clans are patrilineal. There prevails fictional consanguinous kinship among the members of each clan. The Mundas of West Bengal describe clans as *Gotras* and this is possibly due to the Hindu influence.

In course of the fieldwork it was observed that the clans of the Mundas are not strictly exogamous, though they adhere to other conventional taboos and restrictions. In respect of marriage, the members of the tribe emphasize *Banshas,* i.e., lineages. These are considered exogamic units.

Roy also traced the transformation of *Kili* or *Gotra* names as having been due to Hindu influence. Practically the Mundas, because of their prolonged contact with the Hindus, have given up many customs which the other neighbouring communities prefer (eating of beef and pork). This has compelled them even to change their clan names and to come nearer to the Hindu caste system with a definitely better social status. Thus the members of the Chandil (Meteor) clan try to identify them with *Sandil* or Sandilya, a gotra-name of the Hindus, so styled after the sage Sandilya. The members of the Kachim or Kachhua (tortoise) or Kachchap gotra identify themselves with that of Kashyapa, Gotra name of the Hindus, derived from the sage Kashyapa.

Table 3.1

Clan and Totem

Sl. no.	*Clan*	*Totem*
1.	Bagh	Tiger
2.	Bhutkumar	....
3.	Barla	....
4.	Bera	A kind of snake
5.	Chuntia	Rat
6.	Champa	A kind of flower

Sl. no.	Clan	Totem
7.	Chandra	Moon
8.	Chandil	Meteor
9.	Chandal	....
10.	Luti	....
11.	Dhanwar	Strainer to remove chaps
12.	Demta	....
13.	Deuria	....
14.	Ghusur	Pig
15.	Gurcha	A kind of fruit
16.	Guti	Earthen ball for playing
17.	Hemram	A kind of fruit
18.	Harikanki	A kind of bird
19.	Hanaur	....
20.	Hansa	Swan
21.	Haridwar	....
22.	Indur	Rat
23.	Jew	A kind of bird
24.	Jaypakhi	....
25.	Kundulna	....
26.	Kapila	Cow
27.	Kenchua	Earthworm
28.	Kachim	Tortoise
29.	Kashal	....
30.	Karra	Buffalo
31.	Kausalya	A kind of bird
32.	Karapatri	....
33.	Keyata	....
34.	Kuiya	Tiger
35.	Luthi	Small ant
36.	Murud	A kind of flower (plas)
37.	Mugi	Cereal
38.	Madhu	Honey

Sl. no.	Clan	Totem
39.	Nag	Serpent
40.	Nayer	....
41.	Padma	Lotus
42.	Pencha	Owl
43.	Phinge	A kind of bird
44.	Saral	Saral
45.	Sandil	Meteor (?)
46.	Sangor	....
47.	Salmacha	A kind of fish
48.	Surajmukhi	A kind of flower
49.	Snard	Bull
50.	Sirai	A kind of fish
51.	Sili	....
52.	Sapoar	....
53.	Sankha	Conch
54.	Singh	Lion
55.	Tapor	Crown
56.	Taraya/Turkuri	Lotus
57.	Thesa	A kind of bird
58.	Tuti	A kind of flower
59.	Tao	A bird with blue colour
60.	Tirki	....
61.	Ugalsanri	....
62.	Buruili	Mango
63.	Purti	....
64.	Ulda	One kind of tree
65.	Sayaio	....
66.	Dukria	Knee (human body)
67.	Bandra	Monkey
68.	Deogam	A kind of bird
69.	Munduia	Belly (human body)

Table 3.2
Classification of the Totem

Sl. no.	*Classification*	*Dalton (1972)*	*Risley (1892)*	*Roy (1912)*	*Bhowmick (1971)*
1.	Plant		86	10	12
2.	Animal		155	15	29
3.	Heavenly bodies		4	-	3
4.	Inanimate objects		15	-	4
5.	Unclassified		50	11	-
6.	Human body		-	-	2
7.	Not known		28	-	19
	Total		338	36	69

It has been stated earlier that the Bansnas or lineages play an important role in regulating marriage. This lineage is not found among the Mundas of other places. This is only prevalent among the Mundas of the district of Midnapur. During his survey in 15 villages of Midnapur, the author traced 41 clans, of which 24 clans have got only one lineage, 6 clans have 2 lineages each; 2 clans have 3 lineages each; 1 clan has 4 lineages; 1 clan has 5 lineages; 1 clan has 6 lineages; 1 clan has 7 lineages; 1 clan has 9 lineages; 1 clan has 16 lineages; 2 clans have 18 lineages each, and 1 clan has 24 lineages. Particulars of the lineage and clan affiliations have been shown in Table 3.3.

Table 3.3
Clan and lineage affiliations
(Number of sub-lineages is in the parenthesis)

Sl. no.	*Clans*		*Lineages*	*Total*
1.	Nayek		Ghatwal(0)	
2.	Sili		Jabla (0)	
3.	Murgi		Lohahatu (0)	
4.	Kapila		Pameya (0)	
5.	Luti		Sigid (0)	
6.	Murud		Telwari (0)	
7.	Gunrcha		Turda (0)	
8.	Jiw		Bakar Kurid (Keshari) (1)	
9.	Luthi		Sindri (1)	
10.	Harikanki		Chunchuria (1)	
11.	Kachhim		Garakisan (1)	
12.	Bara		Edel	
13.	Ghusur		Kudra (1)	
14.	Guti		Kudra (1)	
15.	Champa		Birgam (2)	
16.	Singh		Burda (2)	
17.	Ugalsnari		Pata (2)	
18.	Kausalya		Saray Bargaon (4)	
19.	Madhu		Satbhaiya (5)	
20.	Kuiya		Kudra (6)	
21.	Taraya		Rela (6)	
22.	Snar		Bakru (7)	
23.	Sirai		Bakru (7)	
24.	Kayta		Bakru (7)	
25.	Chaudal	2	Baradi (0), Patapukuridulmi (3)	
26.	Phinga		Chogalan (0), Bakru (7)	
27.	Sankh		Telwari (0), Harad (5)	

Sl. no.	*Clans*		*Lineages*	*Total*
28.	Padma		Patra (1), Turkundi (6)	
29.	Pencha		Kakru (1), Kakar (3)	
30.	Tuti/Chupi		Buru (0), Kanchi Thakur (2)	6
31.	Suryamukhi	3	Hnesha (0), Karihensa (0), Snebali (6)	
32.	Hemrom		Chhalidajan Lahar Chandamasina (1), Samadi (1), Turda (2)	2
33.	Sandil	4	Hajam (1), Jari (4), Thakur (6), Bakru (7)	
34.	Bagh	5	Atni (0), Hnesla (0), Khemteya (0), Kulajanga (1), Kudra (6)	1
35.	Jaypakhi	6	Datam (0), Jhajri (0), Patar (2), Kadru (1), Changarda (1), Kudra (6)	1
36.	Salmachh	7	Haramro (0), Pel (0), Dadu (1), Gadakisan (1), Silithakur (3), Ardkalithakur (4), Ghagra (5)	1
37.	Saral	9	Ladunb (0), Pata Ashda (0), Udu (1), Sijubarli (0), Tadang (0), Uhatu (0), Rugri (1), Uhstuthakur (2), Bakru (7)	1
38.	Thesa	16	Chakamuri (0), Deuri (0), Icha (0), Ilu (0), Jhajri (0), Masna (0), Chaka (1), Kedaru (1), Sunkarpikiapiri (0), Samadi (1), Patar (2), Buruhatu Chauka (2), Jaj (4), Tunturi (3), sarmali (6), Thakur (6)	1
39.	Chandil	18	Bulungbaradi (0), Khelari (0), Situ (0), Siliroy (0), Tunturi (0), Suisa (1), Chaka (1), Birgam (2), Janbuda (2), Harin (2), Sarjam (6), Harad (5), Satbhaiya (5), Dulmi (5), Thakur (6), Tud (6), Bakru (7), Janumpidibadu (1)	
40.	Tao	18	Bakarkurid (0), Chnar (0), Datam (0), Jagda (0), Londra (0), Marcha (0), Sapa (0), Suri (0), Ganrua (1), Patar (2), Jnabuda (2), Dumura (2), Pata (2), Sar-Jam (6), Chamdu (4), Srmali (6), Thakur (6),	2

Sl. no.	Clans		Lineages	Total
41.	Nag	24	Bansam (0), Chnar (0) Ilu (0), Keda (0), Knidi (0), Kakrudigar (0), Pande (0), Sarugera (0), Sarendi (0), Tutki (1), Chaka (1), Edel (1), Ganrua (1), Saraya (2), Kukru (1), Jnabuda (2), Sarjam (6), Bare (0), Harad (5), Satbhaiya (5), Bukru (7), Baroanr (0), Lota (0)	1
	Total	112		41

It has been observed that most of the clan names are associated with plants, animals, heavenly bodies or inanimate objects, though quite a number of names cannot be meaningfuly understood. But in case of the lineages, where no meaning can be traced, the members of the lineages bear them along with their sub-lineages, if any, with a view to avoiding connubial relationships belonging to the same lineage. This exogamous marriage rule strictly defines the character of the lineages. The members consider that they are related by a common tie of blood relationship and have descended in one line from a common ancestress. According to some old informants, each of these lineage-names has been coined from the women who is regarded as the ancestress of that particular group.

These lineage are not uniformly distributed in all the villages, and there is neither any social hierarchy not any privilege enjoyed by any of the groups.

These lineages, again, have been grouped together according to the number of sub-lineages associated with them. Table 3.4 gives the details of the groupings.

Table 3.4

Grouping of the lineages

Sl. no.	*No. of sub-lineages*	*No. of lineages*
1.	With seven sub-lineages	1
2.	With six sub-lineages	8
3.	With five sub-lineages	3
4.	With four sub-lineages	5
5.	With three sub-lineages	4
6.	With two sub-lineages	12
7.	With one sub-lineages	24
8.	Without sub-lineages	50
	Total	107

The sub-lineages are known as *thok*. The large lineages having many sub-lineages can be referred to as 'maximal lineage'. Table 3.5 gives details of the lineage along with their associated sub-lineages.

Table 3.5

Sub-lineages within the lineages

Sl. no.	*Name of lineage*	*No. of sub-lineage*	*Name of the sub-lineages*
1.	Bakru	7	Lohahatu, Siju, Malida, Todang, Bundu, Haramro, Soma
2.	Rela	6	Sasa, Sarmali, Ludra, Churki, Kushaldi, Chirgaldi
3.	Snebali	6	Suisa, Babuali, Parta, Marcha, Sasa, Patabali
4.	Churki	6	Rela, Kudra, Sasa, Sarmali, Hneseldi, Kushaldi

Sl. no.	Name of lineage	No. of sub-lineage	Name of the sub-lineages
5.	Tud	6	Turkundi, Putkuino, Churiang, Tudturiang, Chudturiang, Tunturi
6.	Turkendi	6	Tud, Tuntuni, Puntkuino, Churiang, Tudturiang, Chudturiang
7.	Kudra	6	Rela, Churki, Sasa, Sarmala, Hneselpi, Kusaldi
8.	Thakur	6	Uhatu, Kali, Syamala, Kanchi, Arkali, Sili
9.	Sarjam	6	Suva, Chuti, Dhadru, Datam, Chuti, Sarjam, Banga, Sarjam
10.	Satbhaiya	5	Samadi, Chuturpa, Paramjareya, Edrong, Anriapata
11.	Dulmi	5	Bongadar, Jeg, Chhatapakhri, Goasidi, Ikir
12.	Harad	5	Suba, Chuti, Tirul, Khiri, Tamaku
13.	Arkali Thakur	4	Kali, Sili, Lohahatu, Uhatu
14.	Jari	4	Gugui, Mugui, Muraguma, Patkam
15.	Chamdu	4	Baragaon, Thorpa, Dadal, Adrapatra
16.	Saray-Bargaon	4	Harat, Kukru, Ilu, Garakisan
17.	Jaj	4	Gamaria, Ichaabaa, Suba, Jaj Bukru
18.	Sili Thakur	3	Silitutki, Katsili, Patsili
19.	Patapukri-Dulmi	3	Baradi, Baksa, Bangadulmi
20.	Tuntuni	3	Bagmuri, Tantan, Turda
21.	Kakar	3	Sapa, Marang, Huding
22.	Buruhatu Chaka	2	Uhatu chauka, Patkam Chauka
23.	Pata	2	Hnesla, Dugda
24.	Burda	2	Bukadi, Uludiri
25.	Dumura	2	Loyadumura, Marangdumura

Sl. no.	*Name of lineage*	*No. of sub-lineage*	*Name of the sub-lineages*
26.	Uhatu Thakur	2	Arkhali Thakur, Sili Thakur
27.	Harin	2	Marang Harin, Banku Harin
28.	Jnabuda	2	Girguri, Gulgu
29.	Kanchi Thakur	2	Bundu, Bakru

It has been said that the Mundas are basically an agricultural community but they have many hunting and fishing appliances just to change the monotony of their agricultural life. Due to growth of population we notice that most of the persons go outside their habitats and settle in new areas, specially in 24 Parganas district, and even have to migrate to Bangladesh and other places. Thus new satellite villages have been formed. Many of them, in their villages, are involve in running petty businesses like selling readymade garments, carpentry and grocery, opening tea stalls or brewing rice beet. Growing and selling of vegetables also help them to a considerable degree. In earlier times the country provided the forest and the forests provided them with fuel, timber, honey, *mahua* flowers, medicinal herbs. Hence in many places, traditional villages are now seldom found. They have become part of the modern socio-economic system. Growth of urbanization has brought many of the Mundas to the industrial centres. All types of economic programming have developed and as a result we find some remarkable changes and these changes have a tremendous impact on their life style. Though the tribal communities are getting many more advantages due to changes in socio-political life, they have brought about some changes in their economic life too. It is true that due to transport facilities and opening of many schools in and around their vicinity, significant changes have been noticed in their life style. However, due to changes in modes of living as well as in socio-political spheres we may expect certain shifts of interest in the traditional life of the Mundas. Practically they are part of the new socio-political situation which has undoubtedly brought about many more changes in their system of education. As a result, their dependence on agriculture has been reduced and a new pattern of economic life has been ushered in.

Rice is the staple food of the Mundas. Generally, meals are taken three times a day. Plenty or green vegetables either from their own field or purchased from the market are consumed by them. Besides, fish, egg, and meat occasionally supplement their food items. Of course, country-made rice beer is also consumed by them. It has been seen that an educated Munda refrains from drinking. The structure and composition of the family, specially in the Munda villages are found to be dominated by simple families, i.e., by parents and unmarried children. In a few cases, old parents stay with the sons when sons are found capable of maintaining themselves. It is to be noted that the old parents also work for the family when the son is grown up and married. These types of families are very common; sometimes they are designed as vertical extended families. There are a few cases of extended families when a few married sons live together under the headship of an old father. Yet it is observed that simple monogamous types of families are dominant in Munda villages. Kiddies are looked after by their unmarried sisters. Divorced or separated persons are approximately less in number and they live with their brothers or sisters as the case may be.

It is important to note that the Mundas of frontier Bengal observe strict rules against marrying within the same 'Bangsha' or lineage. It has been observed that even though they marry within the same clan they never marry in the same lineage or Bangsha. Lineage might be the root of a group of Mundas and their descendants, sub-lineages having different clans. Marriage within the same lineage is strictly prohibited.

In the schedules of marriage ceremonies there are some elaborate rules and regulations. Marriage by negotiations is an orthodox rule in all cases. It has been noted by some that mutual choice or marriage by elopment also take places among them when detailed ceremonies are not arranged. Widow there marriage or *Sangali* is permissible among the Mundas.

Regular marriage as per customs takes place when one *Dutam dar* or 'go-between' is selected and proceeds to negotiate with the marriageable parties i.e., the bridegroom's as well as the bride's. Roy describes the ceremony thus :

> The *Chenri-uri* or omen reading is performed in the following manner. When a Munda father has a suitable bride in view for his son, he sends a go-between called *Dutam* to the guardian of the girl. If the girl's guardian considers the proposal or match desirable, he names a day for *Chenri-uri*. On the appointed day, the bridegroom with two or three relatives, and, if so requested by the girls guardian with the proposed bridegroom too starts for the girls village. On the way, the party go on marking every women good or bad.
>
> If the party happen to come across any bad women on the way they will return home and the negotiations fall through.
>
> (Roy : 1912)

Still this kind of psychological behaviour predominates among the Mundas. Apropos of marriage after the final selection is made, there are certain formalities to be observed. The man who is seeking a suitable bride for his son will visit the house of the parents of a suitable girl. Again, the return visit on the part of the bride's family starts and the wedding day is fixed up. Here, not only the families concerned but also other villagers are involved. Before the finalisation of marriage there is a ritual, when unmarried girls are requested to bring water in a brass cup. Then all senior male members utter the name of the Sun-god who is believed to give the proper direction in the selection of mate. Then, one of the girls is asked to bring two pieces of sun dried rice and two pieces of *durba* grass. The old man in the house is asked to salute the Sun-god and then two pieces of rice are brought and allowed to float in the water kept in the brass cup. The villagers eagerly wait and if they find that the two pieces of sun-dried rice meet or touch each other, then they cheerfully shout and consider that the marriage will be a happy one. Thus the match is finalised and the villagers think it *Dharma Khari,* i.e., settled union as per the desire of God.

Then formal visits and counter visits take place. Father and mother of the bridegroom along with a few old persons of the village visit the house of the bride. Conversely, the parents of the bride and some other people of the bride's village come and visit and finalise the wedding date. They prefer marriage in the month of *Falgun* (Feb-March); of course a few months like *Bhadra* (Aug-Sept) and *Paush* (Dec-Jan) are avoided.

Marriage (Arandi) takes place in the house of the bride. A token bride price amounting now-a-days to Rs. 21.25 paisa is being finalised as the marriage payment. And another sum of Rs. 1.25 paisa is paid to the member of the bride's family. After the formal payment of money, the wedding day is fixed on the third day. A ceremonial marriage booth is prepared where four pieces of banana plants are placed and these are connected with each other by means of a white thread. The bride and the groom are to sit ceremonically facing each other (the bridegroom faces east, the bride west). At that time iron bangle in introduced into the left hand of the bride by the bridegroom. The bridegroom puts vermilion on the forehead and hair parting of the bride and it is done three times. After that two hands are placed on a brass pot on which a betel-leaf is placed and then two hands are tied with a white thread by *Teki* (the priest) belonging to a degraded Utkal Brahmin. Next day the bride and the groom come back to the bridegroom's house with ceremonial flourish. Then the bride and the groom set forth to the groom's house. When they enter the house, the bride and the groom are cordially received by the mother of the bridegroom. Of course, two assistants (one with the bridegroom, a younger boy, and the other with the bride, one little girl) locally known as *Lukundi* are absolutely necessary. Both the bride and the groom come back to the house of the bridegroom and they are received cordially by the mother of the bridegroom who pours water on the feet of the couple by touching their feet. Then the mother kisses the couple and puts sweets in their mouths. Then they are received by the other members and the couple are asked to stay in a room where beddings are prepared. The couple are allowed to change their clothes and go to a tank where they are to take bath. One small brass pot is thrown by the elder sister of the bridegroom and this should be recovered by the bride three times. This ritual is known as *'Kadokhani'*, i.e., playing with mud. Then the couple return to their home. At that time the bride brings one pot of water on her head. She will offer sweets to the groom. When they return to the house, the groom throws an arrow three times into the open space and this is collected back by the grandmother of the bridegroom. When this ritual is over, the younger brother of the groom demands something from the newly-married couple who, in their turn, promise to present something on the day of the marriage of the younger brother. This is repeated three times. Then the couple enter their room. Again, in the house of the bridegroom one wedding platform with four banana plants is prepared, where the newly married couple will sit in a row. Then one elderly female member of the bridegroom's house will keep in a brass plate a few betel leaves, unhusked paddy and sundried rice and six nodules of cowdung. This plate will be taken in front of them and the younger sisters are freely allowed to throw the contents in opposite directions (totally six times). This ceremony is known as *Chuman*, i.e., welcoming or kissing. Then the couple are taken to their home. They slowly start enjoying their normal life, but on the 9th day they will go back to the house of the bride. The ceremony is known as *Firta* which means 'return'. The couple will be in the house of the bride for three days and then come back to the house of the groom. Of course a few members from the bridegroom's family will come to take the couple. Thus, the marriage ceremony is over and the couple will stay permanently as husband and wife with occasional revisits from their relatives.

A small winnowing fan known as *Kata-abreng* is generally used during the marriage ceremony. The bride will hold the winnowing fan and the bridegroom will hold it from behind the bride and slowly move it simulating the act of winnowing. It is generally moved, three times as a part of marriage rite. These are the customs and one has to perform them or to show respect to them if one is not baptised in a church.

VI

Bhumij : Regarding the origin of the Bhumij, Risley (1891) writes :

> Bhumij, a non-Aryan tribe of Manbhum, Singhbhum and western Bengal classed by Dalton and others, mainly on linguistic ground, as Kolarian. There can be no doubt that the Bhumij are closely allied to, if not idential with the Mundas I am inclined myself to believe that the Bhumij are nothing more than a branch of the Mundas, who have spread to the eastward, mingled with the Hindus, and thus for the most part severed their connection with the parent tribe.
>
> I have not been able to discover that the Bhumij possess any independent traditions of migrations. Those who live in the proximity of Chutia Nagpur, recognise no distinction between themselves and the Mundas. They intermarry and associate and coalace in all matters indicating identity of race, for though it may be said that they are not much troubled with caste pryndices, there is no portion of the old Indian population which is quite free from it. The Bhumij father caste have become to Hinduise to acknowledge the relationship. The Dhalbhum Bhumij consider themselves autochthones, and will not admit that they are in any way connected with the Mundas, Hos or Santals. It is pretty certain that the *zamindars* of these estates are of the same race as their people, though the only men among them whom I found sensible enough to acknowledge this was Raja of Bagmundi. Others all call themselves Khatriyas or Rajputs, they do not attempt to connect themselves with any of the recognised families of the tribe but each family has its own special legend of miraculous production.

The sub-tribes are numerous and vary greatly in different districts.

The exogamous divisions of the tribe are totemistic, and closely resemble those met with among the Mundas. The rule of exogamy is simple. A man may not marry a woman of his own sept, not a women who comes within the standard formula for recockming prohibited, degrees calculated as rule to three generations in the discending line, but sometimes extended to five where *bhaiyade* or mutual recognition of kinship has been maintained between the families.

Of course, Risley mentions the titles. These are *Manki* (common with the Munda), *Matkum* (common among the Bhumij of Dhalbhum), *Mura* (common among the Mundas of Manbhum), Sardar. But in Midnapur such titles are absent; all of the Bhumij use Singh as surname as in the case of Munda. Local people classify the Mundas a *Tharua* Bhumij i.e., the group of people who use *Thar* i.e., local dialect. Risley states that they have sub-groups, but these are absent among the Bhumijes of Midnapur. It is interesting to note that members of the sub-groups will never intermarry. Sikharia Bhumij will not marry Tamaria Bhumij. The Bhumij have a good number of septs having a totem. A few examples are the *Badda* sept or clan which has rat as totem, Beghbindha having ox as totem, Ghughu sana having a kind of dove as totem, Sal having a kind of fish as totem, Tesa, a kind of bird as totem, Kashyap having tortoise as totem, Gua Hemrom having betelnut as totem. Bhumij families are patriarchate in nature i.e., they follow the father's line of descent. In actual sense the types of families are very common in many tribes except in the matriarchate Khasi, Garo or the Rabha. Families are nuclear or simple type consisting of parents and unmarried children; another intermediate type of family exists, where we find old parents and married son with unmarried children. Joint family structures are predominant. In a patriarchate family, birth of a son is welcome for it indirectly provides security to the parents. Many more customs are handed down through mutual interaction and training. In socio-religious life the woman has a very significant role to play. Horror of menstruation is dominant in their minds and as such people consider menstrual blood unholy. It is strongly believed that menstrual blood is impure and the touch of a women who has a period is considered to be unclean.

However, they are not allowed to dance with the male persons. They have a traditional political organisation known as the panchayat. They have different office bearers: headman, messenger, priest. The headman is the Mukhia. He has to negotiate for marriage unions. The go-between is known as the *Madhyastha*. Rs. 1.25 is paid for fixation of the marriage date. It is known as the *Lagnadhara*. It is a formality that before the finalisation of the marriage date, the brother's wife of the proposed bride prepare a solution with a little rice powder in water this solution is used for making a floral design. On this design, one brass plate is placed and on it one betel-leaf, one uncut arecanut and some *durba* grass are placed and then a sum of Rs. 1.25 paise is also placed. It is known as *Chumai* i.e., kissing or reception. The wife of the elder brother takes all these in a cup prepared out of *Sal* leaves. Then the conch-shell is blown and on that day, the date and time of wedding are fixed. It is to be remembered that one Brahmin is required to negotiate the finalisation of the marriage date. Only *Bhadra* (Aug-Sept), *Paush* (Dec-Jan) and *Chaitra* (March-April) are avoided. On the day of marriage turmeric paste is anointed on the body and the conch-shell is blown to indicate the auspicious time of marriage. Of course, one day earlier than the marriage day, the bride and the groom are given a feast by their relatives.

They observe certain rules. Betrothal takes place in the house of the bride-elect. Marriage date is fixed by the guardians. Some of the following articles are carried.

(i) *Sari*

(ii) *Blouse*

(iii) One *patkharu* or brass bangle

(iv) Garland

(v) New *ghunsi* or red thread to be tied on the wrist.

The grandmother generally takes the bride on her lap. At the time, the father of the bridegroom ceremonically places the bride price on a plate and this is handed over to the guardian of the bride. Then the actual date and time are fixed. This is known as *Laganbandha,* which is fixed by the parties. After the finalisation of the date of marriage both the bride and the bridegroom become cautious. They do not go outside their own houses. The bridegroom has to keep with him one betelnut cutter made of iron. At the same time the bride has to keep with her one *Kajalpata,* an iron container of collyrium. These are considered to be protectors against any difficulties or dangers. There are other formalities which are performed both by the bridegroom and the bride i.e., anointment of turmeric paste. Senior members initially anoint the bridegroom as well as the bride. At that time conch-shells are blown in both the houses. Then they have to take bath in their respective houses. Some presentations are then given in the form of new clothes or cash money. These are presented to the bridegroom and the bride.

The marriage booth or *Chhamra* is prepared in the house of the bride where the marriage ceremony will take place. The sister's husband has to dig a pit with the help of a hoe and some water is poured into the pit. It is called a *bundh* or tank. Brothers and sisters of the bridegroom cut jokes by sprinkling water from the tank. A yoke with marks or vermilion is generally placed near the *bundh*. The bridegroom has to sit on the yoke. Then, all the attending womenfolk with whom joking relationship is permitted and accepted, stand round the bridegroom with their faces turned back and their have almost touching the face of the bridegroom. Some of them pour water on the heads of the women and the water is gradually poured down on the face of the bridegroom. After that the bridegroom ceremonially has to marry a banana plant. Then he puts three dots of vermilion on the banana plant. The same procedure is followed in the house of the bride. Some Brahman priests from the locality perform the marriage rites. They prepare bangles of thread to which betel nut, unhusked paddy, *durba* grass along with the leaves of mango are tied. One of these bangles for the bridegroom and an other for the bride. The priest ties the bangle on the right wrist of the bridegroom. There are some little ceremonies and ultimately the bridegroom moves towards the house of the bride. On his way, a ceremonial marriage is done with a mango tree on which he puts vermilion marks. He embraces the tree three times. The Brahmin along with the bridegroom and his party starts for the bride's village. The bridegroom is carried by his sister's husband. The bride has to remain blindfolded before the marriage in her room. A cloth is brought for the bride and presented to her along with other ornaments. The bridegroom is carried to the *Chhamra*, i.e., marriage booth. The bride is brought to the booth and taken round the booth three times. Both the bridegroom and the bride are brought and allowed to sit on the lap of the father's brother (bridegroom) and on the lap of the mother's brother (bride) in one row.

After the ceremonial application of vermilion is made by the bridegroom. Three times, of course, the priest utters incantations. Among other formalities, the bridegroom and the bride have to stand facing each other. Apart from the exchange of betels (three times), the corners of the *Sari* and the cloth of the bridegroom are tied by the Brahmin priest. After the ceremony is over the bridegroom and the bride take their seats on a mat. They are served with fried rice, molasses and sweet meats. The marriage party is served with good food and rice beer along with sweet meats. A bridal feast whose menu comprises rice curry and meat is arranged.

At the time of departure from the house of the bride, both the bride and the bridegroom are allowed to sit on a mat. Then a ball of sundried rice and *durba* grass is arranged and the members of the bride's family take this and touch the bride. After the formal performance of touching the cheeks of the bride and the bridegroom, a little cash presentation is made to the bride by the attending relatives. The bridal party leaves the place in a bullock cart. The members of the party are taken to the booth and at that time iron bangle is placed on the right hand of the bride by the bridegroom. A formal ceremony is associated with it. There is one ceremony popularly known as *Lukochuri* (hide and seek). During bath, at the place of the bridegroom's house, the bridegroom has to hide the *Kajallata,* i.e., receptable for callyrium and the bride has to hide the betelnut cutter. Then, after bath, all attending participants have to follow when the bride washes the feet of all the elderly attending members including her husband. Then a feast is arranged. After one day, the bride and the bridegroom start for the bride's village. After two or three days the bride and the groom come back to the bridegroom's village and there they live permanently.

These customs are in vogue in the Bhumij society. Inter-caste marriage is there but the party has to pay fine or arrange for a feast in the presence of the village elders.

VII

Lodha : The Lodhas, a primitive tribal group, mainly live in west Midnapur. Along with them live other tribal communities like the Santal, the Munda, the Kora, the Kharia and the Bhumij. The Lodhas differ physically and culturally from these groups of people; added to this is the stigma of criminality imputed to them by the local people, as well as by the government. Even now, they are deemed as such, and in the event of any theft or dacoity in this area they live in, they are instantly suspected and harassed, both by the people of the locality and by the administrative authorities.

The total number of Lodhas in the state of West Bengal is about 30,000 though the Census department of the Government of India has mixed them up with the Kharias, without any justification. They are concentrated in the district of Midnapur. Some of them are found in the district of Hooghly in West Bengal, Singhbhum in Bihar, and Mayurbhanj in Orissa. They speak a distorted form of Bengali. They live near the outskirts of forests, or sometimes in the fringe of some villages in aggregates of a few families. They are basically a food-gethering people and mainly subsist on collection of wild roots, tubers and edible leaves from the jungles, as also on killing of wild game birds, lizards and alligators which they use as food and whose skins they sell. They also collect *tusser* cocoons, which are sold to a specialised group of people of the weaver community who prepare clothes out of these cocoons. Some leaves specially the leaves of the *kend* trees are collected by them and sold to outside traders, who prepare country-cigars with pounded tobacco mixed with these leaves. They stitch the leaves of Sal trees with thorns and use these as plates for serving food. A large group among them also catch fish and tortoise during the rainy season in the nearby paddy fields or silted tanks of the deforested areas. They also collect faggots from the jungle, make bundles, and sell these in the local market. The money they earn in this way is used to buy the daily necessities of life.

A section of them have migrated to some less forested regions and come into contact with the agrarian communities, from whom they have learnt the art of agriculture. Being thus accustomed to the techniques of agriculture, they now work as day labourers or agricultural workers. But as all these means of earning are not regular and sufficient they face extreme privations in maintaining their families. Moreover, at present they are not getting any facility to make use of the jungle produce as freely as before. Therefore, a large section of them have taken to anti-social activities.

The term 'Lodha' is possibly derived from the Sanskrit word Lubdhaka, meaning a trapper or fowler. There is a land-holding group of people in Madhya Pradesh named 'Lodha'. They are, according to the authorities, immigrants from Uttar Pradesh; they originally belonged to the district of Ludhiana in Punjab. They adopted the appellation 'Lodha' after the place of their origin. According to Nesfield, the name *Lodha* or *Ludhi* has two different derivatives. One is *Lod,* which means 'clod', according to which 'Ludhi' means a clod-hopper. The other is that the Lodhas have adopted their name from the *Lodh* tree, which grows in abundance in northern India, the bark of which is collected and sold by them as a dyeing agent.

The Lodhas take pride in asserting themselves as 'Savara'— a generic term used in ancient literature for the forest-dwelling communities. In the *Ramayana*, we have the episode of Savari anxiously waiting for Ramchandra, who, at that time, was in exile. In the *Mahabharata*, we read about the Kiratas or the Vyadhas, who were the kins of this Savara group of people. According to their traditionally accepted origion, the Lodhas turn out to be the descendants of king Vishwabasu, who once reigned over the jungle tract of the Savara country of Nilachal in Utkal (Orissa). This tribal king possessed the idol of Lord Jagannath, now installed in the famous temple in Puri. Once the king of Puri, Indradumma, was told in his dream that Lord Jagannath wanted to come from his jungle abode and stay in Puri. Then he sent his trusted minister, Vidyapati, who was a Brahman by caste, to secure the idol of the lord. That astute Brahman very tactfully entered Nilachal, the Savara country, made love to Lalita, the endearing and beautiful daughter of the king, and through her help came to know of the actual abode of the lord. Later on, he successfully implemented the plan of stealthily taking away this idol of the lord to Puri. It is said that since then the Lodhas have not paid any respect to the Brahmins. They do not take their assistance in any ritual or ceremony.

The huts of the Lodhas are generally thatched, mudbuilt and of rectangular shape in most of the cases, without any shutters or windows. They have no land of their own, though they use *Khas* or government lands for doing rudimentary agriculture. Now, a few among them, have been given some land by the government for cultivation. They use earthen-ware vessels as cooking utensils. For cutting and felling trees, they use axes and for digging up roots and tubers they use a type of digging spade with a sharp iron-blade, fixed into a wooden shaft.

For hunting purposes, they have bows and arrows. They use various types of basket-traps for catching fish from the shallow streams or paddy fields. The dress worn by the male is very simple, consisting of only a piece of loin-cloth. Now-a-days, however, some of them are using readymade garments. The female wears a *Sari* like other local people, but of a cheaper variety. She uses bangles and a few ornaments of alloy-silver. Females decorate their bodies with tattoos, specially on the foreheads and arms.

The Lodhas are a patriarchate group of people. They consider other tribal communities as 'Adivasis', whereas the rest of the caste Hindu groups are regarded by them as Bangali Babus or Bengali gentlemen or ironically as Knakra. This distinctly separates them from the other groups. The Lodha tribe is grouped into a few exogamous clans. These clans have their respective totems. Each member of the clan pays respect to the totemic object and never kills or injures it.

Table 3.6
Clan and Totem affiliations

Sl. no.	*Name of the clan*	*Totem*
1.	Bhakta	Chirka Alu (A kind of yam)
2.	Mallik	Makar/shark (A kind of sea-monster)
3.	Dandapath/Bag	Tiger
4.	Nayek	Sal fish (Ophicaphalus marulius).
5.	Digar	Porpoise
6.	Ahari	Chanda fish (Ambasis ranga)
7.	Bhunia	Sal fish
8.	Kotal	Moon/Grass-hopper
9.	Paramanik	Manik (A kind of bird)

The Bhakta clan is again subdivided into two groups. One is senior (Bara) and the other junior (Chhota). These clans are patrilineal units. These descend from father to son. After the marriage, the girls give up their father's clan and accept the clan of their respective husbands. The members of the Kotal clan discard and replace their used earthernware vessels on every newmoon day, i.e., when the moon is not seen in the sky. The women of the same clan do not wear conch-sheel bangles.

Most of the families are simple or of the nuclear type, though joint or extended types of families are not rare. In simple families, parents live with their unmarried children, whereas in joint or extended types of families, married sons are found to stay with their parents. There are cases of polygamous types of union, where two wives stay jointly. All the members pool their resources for the upkeep of the family. Marriage by payment of bride-price is the general rule among them. The bridegroom has to pay a bride-price varying from Rs. 3.00 to Rs. 7.00 now a bit more along with some clothes as presentation to the members of the bride's family. Now-a-days instead of paying bride-price the bride's father pays money for the groom in the form of presentation. But the customary bride-price is compulsory. When a girl is married at a tender age, a second marriage ceremony called *Punarbibhaha* is performed after she has attained puberty. In case of offering bride-price, the money is placed on a brass plate by the Sambar, or the chief conductor of marriage. In some places, specially in the jungle areas, on the day of marriage, an alter of clay is prepared, which is brought from under the root of a Sidha tree. At the time of marriage, mother goddess (Basumata) and god of righteousness (Dharam devata) are worshipped. A wedding feast is arranged on the day of marriage, when all the traditional village officials are invited to bless the couple.

Widow marriage is in vogue among the Lodhas. Sometimes the deceased elder brother's wife is married by the younger brother, for which no bride-price is paid and no formal rituals are performed. A sum of Rs. 1.25 paise is paid to the village headman for this type of marriage. This type of marriage is known as *Sanga*. In the *Sanga* form of marriage no vermilion mark is put on the forehead of the propective *Sangali* wife.

The Lodhas have their own tribal council known as the panchayat. The head of the council is known as the Mukhia. The messenger is called the Dakua or Atgharia. His main duty is to intimate the villagers about the particular decisions and directives of the panchayat regarding the village affairs. In a traditional council, personal disputes of the village, and the general problems of village administrations are discussed. This type of panchayat also organises and manages the annual worships and other celebrations. The religious head of the village is known as the Deheri. There are also assistants who help the Deheri at the time of goat-sacrifice. The name of the assistant of the Deheri is *Talia*. In many villages there are sorcerers or magicians, who are suspected by the people for their supposed magical attributes. These magicians have their clients in the villages, far and near. The panchayat decides the cases, when aggrieved persons lodge complaints to them. The panchayat may impose a fine on the offender, or ostracise him, according to the nature of his offence, or take any other deterrent action.

The tutelary village deity of the Lodhas is known as the Baram or Garam. His worship is necessary for the general welfare of the village. If he is aggrieved, they believe that the wild animals will wreak depredations in the village. Besides Baram, they worship goodess Sitala, who is considered to be the controlling deity of epidemic diseases like cholera and chicken pox. They worship her twice a year. Goddess Chandi is also worshipped for cure of chronic diseases. In all the cases, the Deheri, in consultation with the village headman, raises subscriptions and spends the money for purchasing various items needed for the worship. Goddess Manasa is supposed to be the controlling deity of the snakes. Her worship is done only by the snake-charmers of the Lodha community.

At the time of marriage and other celebrations, they propitiate Basumata or mother earth, and Dharam devata or the god of righteousness. But they do not make any sacrifice for their appeasement. They are considered ever beneficial to them. They also believe in various malevolent spirits hovering all about in an unseen form around them. They believe that these spirits control their destiny. For their appeasement, therefore, many rituals are performed and animals are sacrificed. The spirit of Jugini is appeased in a place in the outskirts of the village, where a black fowl is sacrificed.

After the annual worship of Baram or Sitala, communal festivals are held in the village. Their traditional drum is called 'Changu' which is played on, with untiring zest, by expert drummers, and songs composed in distorted Bengali are sung in chorus, accompanied with dance. Their songs are of many types. A few are devotional in nature, in which a good number of popular Hindu gods and goddesses are extolled for their prowess and grace, indicating a slow process of acculturation of Hinduism. There are a few Baramasi songs depicting the episodes of twelve months connected with some heroes of the epic literatures. Besides this, they participate in Tusu festival, which is very common in the western tract of this state. Thus they try to forget the drudgery of their rigid life, their sorrows and tribulations, through rivelry and rejoicing at such celebrations.

It has been stated earlier that the Lodhas have been branded with the stigma of criminality. Prior to the repeal of the criminal tribes act in 1952 , they were considered as a criminal tribe, and later on, as members of an ex-criminal tribe. They were under the purview of this law, for which their movements were restricted, and on the least suspicion, they were arrested and tortured by the police. They were sent to jail for punishment for such supposed criminal activities. It is true that the total number of active criminals among the Lodhas was one-third of the total number of criminals in this district, Midnapur before the revocation of the act. This indicates their nature of criminal propensity. But nobody attempted earlier to find out why such criminality was growing among them. It has been proved that their criminality was due to territorial and economic displacement. As the people lived by food-gathering and by forest produce, they were not in a position to change their mode of life with the change of the circumstances that occurred from time to time. They could not learn the art of agriculture all on a sudden. Rather, they were clamped into a smaller forest territory, which was no more in their possession. Unauthorised entrance into the forest and indiscriminate cutting of the trees were considered punishable by the government and were banned.

Thus all their traditional means of livelihood were suddenly shut out to them, and being left with no other alternative, they chose the path of crime.

The basic causes of crime among the Lodhas still persist. The economically displaced Lodhas could not adopt themselves to the changing situations, which further drove them towards a precarious existence, and the growing needs of an expanding human stock, clamped in a small territory, could not be met with a hewer's income. Persisting frustration and lack of self-reliance brought in their trail perpetual stagnation in their collective life, and subsequently turned them into inveterate criminals, with every knock by the waves of changing circumstances.

The traditional form of political organisation is in disintegrating stage. One old Lodha women sold one young girl to a different caste in Mayurbhanj. The village panchayat questioned the issue but the women and her son left the village. No action was taken.

There are many cases of illicit love with the Lodha women as their husbands are in jail. When a man belonging to the higher caste marries a Lodha woman he has to lose his status. Rather he becomes associated with the Lodha society and is well accepted. There are a good many examples of this type of love case culminating in marriage. But near the urban fringe many Lodha women, without going to their husbands' places prefer to stay in their fathers' village, almost indulging in the life of prostitutes. Still the Lodha people do not object; they understand that it is bad but their village cohesiveness or solidarity is in no way disturbed and no question arises. Naturally, customary laws are disintegrating fast.

However, in traditional marriage ceremonies, some formalities are to be observed. One senior female member goes to the bride's place with five pieces of turmeric, five spoonfuls of mustard oil, new red thread to be worn round the wrist, one wooden bead necklace. It is customary to take them in a new earthen pot. When she arrives at the house of the bride's mother, she receives her with a brass plate containing unhusked paddy and *durba* grass. She sprinkles all these things upon the earthen-pot and receives it with a solutation. It is taken by bride's mother and kept inside. Formal anointment of turmeric paste is continued through five evenings until the marriage takes place. On the occasion of the marriage ceremony a booth is prepared with the placement of four *Sal* posts in four corners covered by palm leaves.

However, the village officials of the Lodhas are :

(1) Mukhia - Headman of the village.

(2) Dakua or Atgharia - Kotal, he belongs to the Kotal clan. He has to work as the village messenger.

(3) Paramanik - He is the village cook and has to cook during celebrations.

(4) Deheri - Village priest.

(5) Talia or Chhardar - Asst. priest.

(6) Hantakar - Official sacrificer.

(7) Besides, there are Byakra or Shaman, and Gunni or medicine man.

Naturally, at present in stall affairs the traditional village council is in a dwindling stage. Most of the newly elected panchayat members belonging to some tribe are to take decisions in respect of violation of the customs.

Chapter Four

DISPUTE—DISSOLVING PROCESSES

I

A human being is a bundle of sentiments and emotions. Besides, many more instinctive forces are there which pull a man or deviate an individual to certain area which might be considered not proper, i.e., against the customs. But certain fomalities developed in the form of tradition, though these might have lacked the written form of law. These are mere customs applicable to society and accepted by all. These are meant as the body of traditional or normative rules which maintain the social order in a particular group specially among the tribal societies and it is true that through these, society is being maintained and cultural life regulated. But society is not static. There are various external forces. At the same time, human groups are not isolated groups in this changing world. As a result, these are the factors on the basis of which society began to change to a certain degree and these changes are perceptible. In the present context after independence, specially in West Bengal where a progressive government is ruling for more than 20 years, the present study has been conducted. Thanks to the new political orientations, by means of greater involvement with them, the people's representatives are trying to bring the rural masses to a certain stage where we may expect many more changes. It has been attempted here to observe how and whether the so-called customary laws are operating in some selected districts of West Bengal. Criminal offences are expected to be dealt with by the police. But it has been observed that the police are more or less statutory and can only follow the dictates of the panchayat or democratic leaders. Many elected persons of the panchayat finalise the issues by discussing them among themselves. Naturally, the local panchayat at the village level is almost supreme, though in some cases the traditional Panchayat is found to deal with issues out of interaction. However, it is generally ascertained that the socio-cultural life of the tribal communities is not disrupting the prevailing law and order situation.

In this chapter attempts have been made to observe the nature of functioning customary laws in tribal societies. At the same time, we have tried to examine how these are dealt with either by the traditional leaders, elected panchayat members or by the court or district law officers. This indicates that the aggrieved party wants a better solution of their problems demands to have a greater justice from the court. This indirectly implies that customary leaders or even panchayat leaders are not doing justice or paying attention to the aggrieved party.

II

In course of our investigations a good number of cases are found in the judicial courts where formal customary laws are not applicable. This indicates that people try to get benefit simply by filing cases against somebody. Some records of these three districts have been sorted out just to get some information on further development of or gradual dissatisfaction with the existing customary rules. Though in earlier times going to the court was not desirable for the community. In this respect Archer's comment is important. According to him, when the case is beyond the village power, as per the gravity of the situation the villagers go to *Pargana* or police just to have solution. But in respect of this study it is to be noted that the Santal customary laws are more powerful than those of the other groups of tribals of the same locality. But in all cases customary laws prevail in settlements of marriage or other extra marital affairs, when the groups concerned try to minimise the magnitude of their transgressions through their village councils.

One case investigated in the court of Chief Judicial Magistrate, Bankura in respect of maintenance of wife (Case no. : 123/1993) is cited here :

> Moyna Soren was living with her working elder sister in Sonamukhi, Bankura. She fell in love with Gopinath Soren and married him in a Kali temple in Sonamukhi. But before this marriage, Gopinath already married a girl. Because of the protest from parents, Gopinath could not keep Moyna with his parents. Gopinath also failed to maintain Moyna. So Moyna had no alternative but to file an application on U/S-125 of the code of criminal procedure of 1973. Gopinath alleged that marriage was not according to the customary law of the Santals and hence it was void. Moreover, as Moyna belongs to the same clan, i.e., Soren, under the Santal customary law the marriage is void at initio. He further contended that as there was no Santal witness it was no marriage in the eye of the Santal law.
>
> On the basis of the oral evidence given by two witnesses the Chief Judicial Magistrate granted the prayer of Moyna and ordered the opposite party, Gopinath to pay Rs. 400 per month as her maintenance allowance. Gopinath has preferred a revisional application before the honourable

High Court of Calcutta where it is still pending for decision.

Another example of civil suits as non-Santal Vs. a Santal. Title suit no. 95 of 1988 in the Court of Munsif, Khatra - Bankura is as follows :

> Basudev Patra, a non-tribe alleged that the possession in plot no. 320 and 321 in Mauja Surulia was being threatened by Prasad Soren and other members of his tribal group. He pleaded that by virtue of an oral exchange with the defendant's fathers, his father got the property and the record of right was also in favour of his father. Hence, he prayed for declaration of title in the plots and permanent injuction against the tribes man.
>
> The suit decreed in favour of the plantiff, Basudev against Prasad Soren and other tribesmen. This suit shows that a non-tribe has brought the Santals to the court of law. The witnesses who deposed for Prasad Soren could not defend and prove by which right Prasad was cultivating and possessing the land, but the fact remains that Prasad and other Santals were possessing the land for long time. Due to lack of vigilance the Santals did not keep the records of their lands and hence lost the suit.

Suits - *Santal vs. Santal:* Another classification can be made, of the civil suits, involving disputes among the tribal members themselves. T.S. 59/911 in the court of the Munsif, Jhargram, Midnapur, Chand Murmu filed this suit against Durga Hansda, his sister and other relatives, when they were claiming right and title over his father's property. His father also gifted him a larger share for the eldest son, they were not recognising it. The matter was primarily settled by the council in favour of Chand Murmu. The Manjhi ruled that the sister had no right/interest in the

> property of her father when there were male heirs. The council's decision did not satisfy Durga Hansda and his relatives.

The suit is still pending in court.

Thus it is abundantly clear that only the Santals follow and do not try to violate the customary laws which are still prevalent among themselves except among the converted Christians.

Against this background we like to discuss the nature of violation of laws in all the communities under survey.

III

Many more cases were reported and all of them were studied with reference to the tribes, Santal, Mahali, Kora, Kharia, Munda, Bhumij and Lodha. Considering so many similar type of cases, attempts have been made to describe only 100 cases from all the tribes under survey. Out of these a few cases have been dealt with by the community council, some of them have been referred to the elected panchayat - and in a few cases the aggrieved parties have gone to the court. This reflects the functioning of the customary laws among the tribal groups we have considered.

Reports reflect the total number of cases considered to be worthy or mention. Out of 100 cases 58 have been dealt with by the elected panchayat, 29 cases have been discussed by their respected community councils and 13 cases from different community groups have been referred to the court. Table 4.1 depicts the communities and the modes of dealing with the cases.

Table 4.1

Communities and the cases

Sl. no.		*By community*	*By the elected panchayat*	*Court*	*Total*
1.	Santal	7	19	4	30
2.	Mahali	3	9	1	13
3.	Kora	7	6	1	14
4.	Kharia	5	2	-	7
5.	Munda	3	10	3	16
6.	Bhumij	1	11	3	15
7.	Lodha	3	1	1	5
	Total	29	58	13	100

Santal: One Suklal Hemrom of Murakata under the Police Station of Narayangarh, Midnapur had picked up quarrels with his five brothers in connection with a plot of land five years ago. The matter was not finalised among themselves. Automatically it was referred to the village council. But the village elders, getting the requisite information, finalised the matter, dividing the plot of land into five parts and none objected to the decision of the community panchayat.

During an annual worship in a village a few persons began to quarrel as a consequence of over-consumption of countrymade rice beer. Soon they lost their temper and began to beat each other. The village headman was present and he immediately convened the panchayat on the spot and settled the dispute. Those who were involved in fighting were asked to stop their quarrel and compelled to apologise before the caste council for their misconduct.

In the village Murakata of Narayangarh Police Station, Midnapur, three sons of Lakshman Hemrom started fighting with one another after consuming rice beer. Of course, there was a cold strain in connection with a patch of land belonging to their ancestors. One of the brothers wanted to get more and there was no alternative but to go to the village council. The Manjhi and other elderly persons of the village assembled in the house of Lakshman Hemrom and made a decision. They wanted to defy the verdict of the traditional village elders. The elected panchayat was informed, but one of the brothers disobeyed their verdict. Ultimately Lakshman Hemrom filed a suit on this issue to the court. The case is pending for decision.

Few years ago the villagers of Murakata proposed to organise an annual festival with the mutual co-operation and help of the village Mukhia and the Manjhi. Anyway, the Manjhi scolded a boy for not performing his duty. He became angry and losing his temper began to abuse the Manjhi and both got involved in a quarrel. The Manjhi felt insulted on account of the incident and wanted to tender his resignation from his post. On hearing this the villagers rushed to the house of the Manjhi and requested him to withdraw his resignation on the condition that the guilty should apologise openly. The villagers compelled the young boy to apologise before the villagers. The Manjhi then withdrew his resignation.

About two years ago, in the same village of Murakata, a young Santal boy named Pilchu Tudu fell in love with a girl and their love continued for a few years. Of course, they married, arriving at the place of the village deity. The family members of the girl had no consent. When they were intimated, they simply ignored the fact. Rather, the girl's family members arranged her marriage at Binapur about 10 kms. away. The marriage took place but the girl did not want to stay with the man whom she had to marry officially. Once when she was in the village, she fled away and came back to Pilchu's (i.e., her first husband's) house. When the news got a wide publicity the second husband who married her, complained to the village council against Pilchu for eloping with his wife. Ultimately the village council met and discussed the whole problem. They finalised that Pilchu was the main culprit and as such the council fined him a sum of Rs. 5000 and this amount was to be given to the second husband. Pilchu managed to sell his land and paid Rs. 5000 to the man, who then went back.

Ramlal Hemrom of Benji, P.S. Narayangarh, was a forest labourer. One Gobinda Soren used to work in the forest office as a night guard. Ramlal Hemrom fell in love with the daughter of Gobinda Soren. One day, Ramlal eloped with the girl and took her away to his sister's place which was located about 20 kms. away from this village. When Gobinda Soren and his wife came to know about the incident, Gobinda's wife was not at all satisfied with what Ramlal had done and compelled her husband to lodge a complaint to the Manjhi against Ramlal. The Manjhi, along with some elderly persons of the village, called a meeting to solve the problem. Ultimately the panchayat came to the conclusion that Ramlal was guilty, but they agreed to let him go because it was his first offence and decided that he would have to pay a fine as compensation to the girl's parents.

One Nabakumar Baske of Jhilimili, in the district of Bankura of Ranibandh, quarrelled with his brother for his parental property. Ultimately it was reported to the village panchayat who settled the matter amicably. In the same village of Jhilimili, one Nagen Hansda occupied a plot of land owned by Matu Murmu. Nagen did it cleverly because he knew that Matu Murmu did not have any document to testify to his ownership of this land. The panchayat was informed of the matter and they amicably and properly settled the case, championing the right cause. Nobody had any reason to complain.

In the same village of Jhlimili, under Bankura district, Naren Hansda used to live with his elder brother who had four sons, namely Arjun, Bijoy, Santa and Bhim. After the death of his elder brother, Naren purchased a plot of land its cost being borne both by Naren and the sons of his elder brother. Of course, Naren had to pay the highest amount as he was in service and had money. After his retirement, he wanted to be separated from his joint family. The property was registered in his name alone and he wanted to exercise exclusive rights on it. It was objected to by Arjun and his brothers. As a result of the dispute, a case was lodged to the village panchayat. But the decision of the panchayat could not satisfy them all. The aggrieved party went to the court for proper justice. The case is still pending.

One Nirmal Besra of Raotora village under Ranibundh of Bankura district was cultivating a plot of land for a long time. Another Gobinda Hemrom of the same village had an eye over his plot of land. Somehow he managed to get this plot recorded in his deeds. Thereafter, when he went to take the possession of the land, Bimal Besra and his family members prevented him from doing so. Both of them got involved in a quarrel. The case was reported to the gram panchayat. It has not yet been decided.

One Ananda Kisku of Banspahari village under Binpur of Midnapur, sold a plot of land to one Ajit Kishku who came to cut some trees grown on the plot of land. But Ananda Kisku prevented him from cutting and felling the trees and demanded extra money for those trees. Ajit Kisku refused to pay as the trees were on the plot of land which he had purchased. He considered the trees as his own as the plot of land belonged to him. But Ananda was of opinion that he had sold to Ajit Kisku that plot of land only but not the trees grown on it. The quarrel intensified and they went to the gram panchayat which later on settled the dispute.

One Sumanta Besra of Muchikara village under Ranibandh of Bankura district, married one Kajol. He demanded one bi-cycle from his father-in-law. His father-in-law agreed to meet his demand but ultimately he failed to keep his promise within a span of five years after his daughter's marriage. Sumanta repeatedly requested him directly or through his wife. But his father-in-law failed to oblige him. This ultimately resulted in a conflict between husband and wife. They were gradually involved in a fieree quarrel. Sumanta's wife, Kajol, informed her father about the whole incident. Thereafter some relatives of Kajol and Sumanta visited the party office where the pradhans of the two villages settled the matter amicably.

In the same Muchikata village, one day Shyam Kisku went to Burdwan for some work and remained absent for a long period from his house. His wife, Dhanamani, developed an illicit relation with one young man of the same village. On his return to the village, Shyam Kisku came to know the whole story related to his wife. It automatically infuriated him and involved them in quarrels which took place off and on. Unable to bear her husband's insulting reproaches and his cruel behaviour she appealed to the party (CPIM) members to save her from her husband's anger as well as from his occasional torture. Ultimately a meeting was convened by the party members in the gram panchayat office where Shyam and his wife Dhanamani Kisku were present. The case was ultimately settled and nothing had to be paid by the couple as token punishment.

One Rabindra Mandi of Gulpara village under Ranibandh Police Station in the district of Bankura married one Sonali Mandi. After a few years in the relation between husband and wife some sort of dissatisfaction began to crop up and Rabindra started disliking his wife. Very surreptitiously, he developed intimicy with another woman of the same village. The secret was gradually leaked out and it went upto the ear of Sonali. Ultimately there developed a severe conflict between husband and wife. At first, some of the relatives and a few villagers tried to intervene and settle the matter. But their decision could not change the behaviour of Rabindra. So Sonali again appealed to the gram panchayat which ultimately settled the case.

Mahali : Ghatu Mahali and Paresh Mahali lived in the same village in the district of Midnapur. Gradually three *Kathas* of land belonging to Ghatu was forcibly occupied by Paresh Mahali of the same village. After possessing the land Paresh began to keep his domestic animals there. Ghatu requested Paresh to vacate his land, but Paresh refused. Facing difficulty Ghatu approached the villagers and narrated the whole story. But the community panchayat did not pay any attention to what he said. Then he went to the village panchayat who settled the matter in his favour.

Subhadra Mahali and Radhi Mahali were neighbours who lived together for a longtime. One day, their sons involved themselves in a quarrel which ultimately produced strained relations between the two families. Ultimately, one day, the quarrel of the sons reached such a stage that they began to fight each other. The neighbours had no alternative but to go to the party office. The party members removed the bitterness and thus temporary compromise took place.

One Raban, a Mahali woman, was alone in her cottage. She used to live in one side of a house owned by a different man. One day, when all members of the house were away, Raban was raped by the owner of the house. Then she was crying. Hearing her cry, people from the neighbourhood crowded and began to beat the miscreant. Ultimately the villagers took the matter to the village panchayat which fined him a heavy amount for his misdeed.

One Mahakum Mahali used to beat his wife regularly. Of course, he was a man who regularly consume country beer. His wife, Malati, reported to the neighbours and ultimately some village elders decided to have a direct evidence. As usual Mahakum, coming back from the market, began to beat his wife Malati. He was totally drunk. Then the neighbours of Mahakum lodged a complaint to the party office. The party members intervened and Mahakum was fined. The fine was paid immediately.

One Kalipada Mahali was involved in a quarrel with his wife Bharati. Bharati, becoming angry, left her husband's house and went straight to her father's village which was situated within a radius of one kilometer. She did not show any intention of coming back to her husband's place. Kalipada, waited for the return of his wife, but she did not come back. Some relatives of Kalipada went to the house of Bharati's father, where a few village elders were asked to be present, there Kalipada promised that henceforth his wife would never be beaten. If he ever violated his promise he would accept any sort of punishment from the village council.

Sometime in 1985 one Bamdev Mahali sold 18 dec. of uncultivated land to one Ram Gopal Mahato of a nearby village at Rs. 120. But later on Mahato came to know that the land of a tribal group could not be sold without having the necessary order from the government. He appealed to the panchayat for return of money which had been given to the owner. The panchayat directed the owner to return the money as per the application of the purchaser, Sri Gopal Mahato. Naturally the dispute was amicably solved when the owner paid back the amount which he had taken.

One Rajani Mahali was a *Gunin* - i.e., magician. Binode Mahali was his neighbour. Binode gradually developed an idea that Rajani, by virtue of his magical potential, could do any sort of harm to his wife as they were not on good terms. One day she abused Rajani. Rajani felt very much insulted and appealed to the village council. All the villagers came and they suggested that Binode should apologise publicly. Thus the villagers brought peace to the village.

Once a Santal boy from a nearby village lifted a fowl from the house of Matilal Mahali. One or two days later Motilal smelled that the fowl had been stolen by a Santal boy. Then Matilal lodged a complaint to the party office. Accordingly, the party members and some panchayat members convened a meeting. On interrogation the Santal boy confessed that he had committed theft. The party members fined him. A sum of Rs. 30 was paid by the Santal boy to the party office and Rs. 20 to the owner of the fowl.

Shripati Mahali of the village Muchikata of Bankura was involved in a quarrel regarding the division of his parental property. The brothers had a little quantity of land for agricultural operations. Shripati brought the matter to the notice of the panchayat which finally convened a meeting on the issue and made a very amicable settlement. For this nobody had to suffer any grievances. Thus the Panchayat members played a very important role in managing the village affairs.

One Nemai Mahali of the village Palgaria, Midnapur, suspected one Purnachandra Mahali of the same village of stealing his paddy. The weight of the paddy was approximately 20 kgs. After hearing his complaint the panchayat members made investigations and came to the conclusion that the complaint was not unfounded. Then the Panchayat convened a local meeting where all the contending persons were present. After cross-checking and interrogations the case was decided. The man confessed his guilt. The panchayat imposed on him a fine of Rs. 25. It was paid by the accused immediately.

One Haru Chakravorty of the village sold his little land to Bari Mahali of the village Banshala of Bankura. Bari Mahali, after purchasing the land, saw that one Sanatan, a non Mahali, had been occupying the land for a long time. Sanatan did not vacate the land and did not show any papers about his possession right. When Bari did not find any alternative he went to the party office for justice. And justice was meted out to him accordingly.

One Ramen Mahali of the village Noapara, Midnapur, embarked on the marriage negotiations of his daughter, Parul, with a young man named Hoplu. Hoplu paid Rs. 50 to the father of the bride. But some troubles cropped up. Parul did not like Hoplu as a suitable groom for her. Naturally, she refused to stay with Hoplu. Ultimately it was found out that Parul had fled away with a young man named Sumanta. This incident made Romen Mahali and his wife very angry. They severed all relations with Parul. Knowing the grievances of Hoplu, the maternal uncle and the husband of Parul expressed their desire for a mutual settlement. Ultimately, because of the interference of the local political party, a settlement was made and thus the grievances of Hoplu were dissolved.

However, it is found that the disputes of the Mahalis are not enormous in nature. As they are poor, their grievances are small and these are settled either by the local party members or by their own village council.

Kora: One Biju Singh of the village Lotanpara, P.S. Narayangarh was working as a day labourer for more than the last 10 years. During his stay there, he fell in love with a Santal girl. Later on, they married. After the marriage, the Manjhi of the groom's village demanded a fine for marrying the Santal girl. According to him, this marriage was against the custom. As a violation of the customary rule, this union should not have taken place. But the decision of the panchayat was not accepted by Biju, the Kora boy. He objected to the decision of the panchayat. As a result the couple did not come back to their respective villages, rather they decided to stay at Mecheda railway station where they would work as day labourers. Naturally the panchayat was not in a position to realise the fine. Automatically, the husband and wife were ostracised by their respective village councils.

Another Atul Singh of the same village had three sons. After the marriage of the first and second sons, he began to cultivate the land owned by the third son, who was the youngest one. The first two sons wanted their shares for the cultivated land, but Atul refused to give them anything as the land belonged to his third son. But the two brothers went to the village panchayat and reported that the third son was not there to claim his share. Their father should equally distribute the land and other brothers should get their shares. When the case was reported to the panchayat, the panchayat leaders discussed everything in detail. Atul should to distribute the land among all his sons but he categorically refused to past, with the land in his possession. The panchayat could not go against the will of Atul. But the two brothers forcibly started to cultivate the land of Atul, ignoring their father. Atul, without seeing any alternative, filed a suit to the court against his two sons for illegal occupation. The case is going on in the court.

In the village Biakudea, under the P.S. of Baraban in the district of Purulia, one Kora celebrated the *Garam puja* in which male folk generally participate. Of course, subscriptions were generally collected from the villagers. When the organisers of the festival committee went to collect subscription from one Budhi Munda, he expressed his inability to comply with their request. In spite of repeated demands for the subscription Budhu Munda stuck to his decision as he had no capacity to pay subscription. Then the organisers made a complaint to the panchayat which convened a meeting and ordered Budhu to pay his subscription. Budhu again expressed his inability to contribute the subscription due to his financial hardship. The members of the panchayat were not satisfied with his reply. They boycotted him and detaching him from the village community, severed all connections with his family. Hearing the verdict of the panchayat, the eldest son of Budhu rushed to the members of the panchayat and proposed that they would pay the amount fixed by the panchayat as subscription. He also prayed to the panchayat to withdraw their decision so that they might get back their social position in the village community. Ultimately, the panchayat agreed to the proposal and thus a mutual settlement took place.

Sometime in 1994, Biru Mudi of the village Biakudra in the P.S. of Burubazar of Purulia district lodged a complaint to the panchayat against one Shyam Mudi who had stolen one cock of Biru. It was killed and eaten surreptitiously. He also complained that while he was searching the cock, one of the young boys of the village informed him that the cock was caught by Shyam Mudi who had killed and consumed it. On further enquiry equity Biru discovered the feathers of the cock strewn over the ground a little away from Shyam Mudi's house. On hearing his complaint the panchayat convened a meeting. They asked Shyam Mudi to be present in the meeting where they charged him for this act of theft. Ultimately Shyam Mudi confessed that he was guilty. He bowed down and touched the feet of Biru, requesting him to excuse him for his fault. He also apologised to the panchayat and again repeatedly requested them to forgive him for the first time. Ultimately, the panchayat members pardoned him.

Ranjit Mudi and Siron Mudi are two inhabitants of the village Rautaca, P.S. Ranibundh, Bankura. Over the possession of some Mahua trees, they came into conflict with each other, which finally resulted in beating and exchange of harsh and filthy words. Ultimately Ranjit Mudi lodged a complaint against Siron Mudi to the panchayat. The panchayat convened a meeting accordingly. They allowed the two contending parties to defend and to give statements before the panchayat. After due hearing from both sides, the matter was mutually settled.

Kharia : Altogether 7 cases of disputes have been found among the Kharias who are a gathering-hunting tribe, mostly dependent on collection of roots, tubers and faggots. They have a formal caste council. Besides, there is an elected gram sabha. Some elderly Kharia are represented in the panchayat.

One Baneswar Sabar of Banskanali, P.S. Ranibundh of Bankura picked up a quarrel with the village council in connection with the fixation of the subscription for the annual Garam Puja. The Mahalis also participate in this festival. The quarrel between the two groups created crises. Then all the villagers made a compromise and politely submitted that they were poor and hence unable to contribute the amount which was fixed by village council. Other villagers paid attention to this situation and agreed to strive a compromise as there was no alternative.

One Sibu Sabar intentionally put a vermilion mark on the forehead of Bhadri, a young unmarried girl. There was protest on the part of the girl's family but due to the pressure exerted by all the villagers this was considered as nothing short of marriage as the women involved did not make any complaints. The village council took up the case, considered it insignificant and finalised it by mutual consent.

Two cases were discussed by the members of the elected panchayat where not only the Kharias but also the Mahalis and other tribal groups participated. The cases were related to the cutting of trees. The tree and the land belonged to man of the non-Kharia group. The Kharias warned him and ultimately the aggrieved party reported the matter to the village panchayat. The panchayat warned him for the misdeed and fined the man who was involved in cutting the trees. Another case of the same nature was reported to the panchayat which convened a metting. All elected members participated in the meeting.

It is important to note that the Kharias, a primitive tribal group, have very little assets of their own. Besides, the group of people have very inadequate interactional scope with the neighbouring communities. So their formal panchayat has a rather insignificant role to play.

Munda : About fifteen years ago trouble and conflict developed in connection with a village worship, i.e., Sitalapuja at Pichabani, Midnapur. The organising committee of the puja fixed up a certain amount as subscription to be given by all the villagers equally. But a few villagers protested against this decision. They were of opinion that the amount fixed as subscription was too much for them. There were some poor persons in the village. Naturally the decision should be changed. The committee rejected their appeal on the ground that this was the only puja where all people take part. Ultimately those who protested decided to boycott the puja. The puja committee became arrogant and were not interested in amicably settling the matter. As a result, another group also made arrangements for a separate puja. One Srikanta Singh, a government employee, took the initiative and solved the problem. After that the village unity was re-established.

One Suraj Singh, an employee of Kharagpur railway workshop, went to Jalipadima to attend a marriage ceremony along with his friend. There he found one young healthy girl named Pratima. They were attracted to each other and intimacy developed between them. Later on, they met several times on many occasions. However, after the wedding ceremony they got ample scope and opportunity to stay together and thus they came closer to each other. He felt tempted to apply vermilion mark on her forehead. Pratima did not object to this. But the relatives of Pratima and many other villagers became angry. They though that Suraj had humiliated them. Automatically they began to quarrel. Suraj and his friends were stronger and soon they began to beat the relatives of the girls. At that time, some relatives of Pratima went to the police station to lodge a complaint against Suraj and his friends. The police appeared on the spot and found Suraj guilty. Suraj was subsequently arrested. A complaint was lodged to the railway authorities who gave him employment. Ultimately he had to lose his job.

One Bagh Singh of Pichabani village under the police station of Narayangarh, and one Malati Singh of Sarisha village used to work together. They came closer to each other. They finally decided to marry against the consent of Malati's father, Sanata. When Sanatan came to know of their decision, he objected to it. But Bagh Singh took Malati to his house and began to live together as husband and wife. The pradhan of the village called a meeting in order to settle the matter. Bagh Singh arranged for entertainment with sumptuous food. The panchayat along with some influential party members participated in the function. Sanatan, father of Malati, did not take part in it, rather he expressed his anger in a different way. As the panchayat was in favour of this marriage nothing untoward took place. Ultimately after a few years an amicable settlement was made. Malati went to her father's place and shed tears before her parents.

In the village Paturia under the Narayangarh P.S. there are six Munda families. Every year they used to worship Baram. All the villagers participated in the Puja. Rana Singh of the same village had two daughters, but due to his illness, he stayed in his elder daughter's place. He died there, but the elder daughter did not invite the other villagers to the funeral feast which she organised, though a few of her choice friends and relatives were asked to participate in this ceremony. This behaviour displeased some influential Mundas who expressed their anger. The village Mukhia or headman was reported and he understood their grievances. The village elders took the matter seriously and considered it as an example of the violation of an accepted custom. All the villagers were not invited to participate in the village worship next year. After that the entire village was divided and still now no compromise has taken place. The elected gram panchayat did not interfere in the matter. Gradually two worships in the village have been arranged as the Mukhia felt insulted. In spite of the dominating CPI(M) members, the villagers have not been able to force the other villagers to surrender. As a result, the village has lost its integrity, the village council has been bifurcated and the elected village panchayat remains silent.

Bhumij : Altogether 15 cases in respect of Bhumij tribe have been collected. Of these one case was decided by the community council, 11 cases were decided by the elected Panchayat and one case was referred to the court.

Ajit Singh Sardar of the village Kutra in the district of Purulia faced opposition when he wanted to organise Sarhul festival. Through four generations he had been the 'Laya'. Due to his position he used to make animal sacrifice before the village deity and as usual he took the lion's share. This was opposed by some other people of the village. Besides, he did not give a proper account of the expenditure incurred at the time of the festival. Thus he gradually lost his status and position and became unpopular. Automatically, the village elders joined together and removed Ajit Singh from the post of 'Laya', i.e., village priest, and elected Mathur Singh as 'Laya' and requested him to perform all ceremonial activities. In spite of all these, Ajit Singh tried his best to take to propaganda in his favour but got little support from the villagers. Thus he lost his case because most of the villagers did not support him and the community council changed their custom of clinging to the hereditary post of the Laya, i.e., village priest.

There are 11 cases or disputes. These were referred to the elected panchayat, indicating that the traditional caste council gradually lost their strength or rather the party-dominated panchayat superseded the caste council.

One Chaitak Singh Sardar of Purulia refused to give his property to his son who was married. The facts were very simple. After the marriage, his son began to torture his wife i.e., the daughter-in-law of Chaitak. This was opposed not only by his family but by others also. Naturally, his father lodged a complaint to the village council dominated by the CPI(M) and composed not only of their own caste members but also of some other groups. Ultimately, the village panchayat fixed up a date for preliminary discussion but it was not finalised, the date being shifted.

One Kumud Singh Sardar of the village Serenga, Bhumij para in the P.S. of Ranibundh, Bankura, was out of his house. At that time, his neighbour Dhananjay entered his house and exchanged hot words with his wife because he was in an intoxicated condition. He began to beat her also. Neighbouring families came to the spot and protested. Ultimately this was reported to the party-dominated village panchayat. The *Soloyana*, i.e., formal sitting took place and the village council dominated by the party, fined Dhananjay for this disagreeable behaviour. He had to pay a fine to the panchayat and apologise for his misdeed.

A conflict in connection with the possession of land arose with one Santal and one Bhumij of the village Suitari of P.S. Ranibundh, Bankura. This was reported to the police station and ultimately the village panchayat took the case, but it has not yet been settled.

In another village Bhudrudanga, P.S. Ranibundh of Bankura, Sudhir Singh Sardar had been cultivating a plot of 33 dec. All on a sudden one Biswanath Mallick started ploughing the land. Sudhir immediately lodged a complaint to the party office. The members of the party made a compromise and warned Biswanath.

A familial conflict on the grounds of possession of land and its cultivation right by the mother-in-law and her daughter-in-law was reported to the village panchayat of Bansdiha under the police station of Ranibundh, Bankura. As there was no male member in the family, the widowed daughter-in-law sought partition with her mother-in-law. This conflict came to its peak in regular quarrels when a few interested persons from both the sides provoked them. But due to the interference of the party panchayat it was stopped and an amicable settlement was made. The interested persons slowly disappeared and a stable compromise was achieved.

Such was a case in the same village of Bansdiha, in Bankura. There were a few disputes also but due to the interference of the party members a compromise took place. One Mahendra Singh of Hijla, Bankura, had 0.75 dec. of cultivable land and this was cultivated by him. Mahender Singh has no issue. Naturally many interested persons were vigilant enough to devise as to how this plot of land could be occupied. One clever Mahato came into the picture and he forcibly ploughed the land with the idea that nobody would oppose him as he was supported by the ruling political party. Ultimately, Mahendar Singh did not find any alternative and as such went to the court to seek justice.

Thus, it is observed that among the Bhumij, the elected panchayats have a dominant role and all sorts of disputes are tackled by the elected members. Their caste council has no role at all.

Lodha : There are altogether 5 cases reported from the Lodhas who are gathering-hunting people. 3 cases were settled by the caste council, one was solved by the elected village panchayat and one was reported to the court. Of the three cases, one was related to the cutting of trees by a Lodha. The villagers protested against this as they did not approve of this type of cutting trees. Naturally, the village council insisted that the involved Lodha should apologise and thus a mutual compromise was negotiated.

Another case was of a young miscreant Lodha young man who surreptitiously entered the garden of a man. He was found to pluck guavas. The owner reported the matter to the village elders who formally warned him. One of the senior members of the village has beat him publicly for such a wrong deed and he was also asked to apologise publicly. But he was not fined.

Another young Lodha boy stealthily entered a nearby hostel room and removed some belogings of an outsider. He was identified by his shoes as these were found near the door. The village headman was intimated and ultimately all the members of the village council convened a meeting where the man apologised, but a few senior persons beat him on the spot. All the belongings were returned to the outsider, but no fine was imposed on the boy as it was beyond his capacity to pay it.

Another case concerned the land distribution by the state government in connection with rehabilitation. Indra Bhakta used to stay with his youngest son - who was at that time a minor. Other sons had their separate establishment; they got free land from the government quota. Naturally the youngest son who was not grown-up, was not given any share. After the death of Indra Bhakta his other sons claimed their shares. The village panchayat said that the father's land should be distributed equally among all his sons. But some other persons of the neighbourhood said that the youngest son, i.e., Mangal Bhakta should go to the Revenue Officer attached to the Scheduled Cast and Scheduled Tribe welfare department and narrate everything. Ultimately, the officer-in-charge came to the spot and said that the land enjoyed by Indra Bhakta was given by the government. As the youngest son of Indra Bhakta did not get any share and as he was a minor at that time, the land which was given to Indra Bhakta should be automatically handed down to his youngest son, i.e., Mangal Bhakta. Thus the dispute was settled.

IV

While explaining various forms of customary laws it is found that among the above-mentioned tribal communities we do not have any parity in them. These differ from tribe to tribe. For the Bengali speaking tribes like the Bhumij and the Lodhas, the forms of the laws are not uniform. In the case of the Bhumij practically no formalities exist; their system of exerting the laws is as per the local democratic set-up. Such is the case of the Lodhas. But they stick to some of their traditional customs, though we find in them examples of Hinduisation. Tree marriage before the actual marriage procedure is a must. Besides, divorce and remarriage have little precedence. After the divorce, a woman is entitled to have a second husband as per her term and thus second marriage is known as *Sangali Bar*. If the first husband is alive, the woman (after divorce) will continue to have the vermilion mark on her forehead. Even if the *Sangali* husband dies, she will still put the vermilion mark on her forehead. Only after the death of the first or married husband she may not have anything to do with vermilion.

We like to clarify the point that customary laws vary from place to place and from tribe to tribe - though the force of Hinduisation is there. It is to be noted that the converted Muslim as well as Christian women, after their marriage, are found to have vermilion marks on their foreheads as a sign of marriage, and nobody objects to this practice.

Our discussion makes it clear that there are certain tribes who adhere strictly to their customs and other associated forms of life. Of course, the tribals in the midst of caste Hindu groups or even after conversion, find their customs change at different degrees. The changes depend on the situations and the nature of variation is also not uniform. This is due to local adjustment. As a result the operation of the laws varies and we have to accept such variations. Bride price and marriage by elopement vary from tribe to tribe. It is observed that some groups like the educated Mahalis do not pay any formal bride price, but a token amount is to be paid to the bride's mother or her family, as it is customary. Thus the customs survive at different degrees and it becomes very difficult for them to overcome these customs. Penalties, as per custom, in marriage and marital involvements are in many cases strictly adhered to in an orthodox pattern. In all these cases, the native law dominates in the region. It is also seen that the tribals are not satisfied until the offender gets punishment through a systematic procedure. Here it is to be remembered that in all these tribal communities justice is considered to be indigenous and local and it suit the genius of the people. These groups of tribals take due notice of their social taboos and customary usages. In fact, these are the products of customary laws. As we see, they preserve the customary laws by their regular application and proper interpretation. The tribal groups can better understand and appreciate this system of justice. As the systems of justice have evolved from the popular consciousness, the participation of the groups in them is very high. Such systems of justice are necessarily simple and cheap. The system of local justice is not unknown among the tribal communities of the world. In ancient India, similar local institutions for the administration of justice did exist. In the *Smritis* there are reference to popular village courts, like family court and village court.

V

It is to be remembered that these institutions of justice are far more prompt in administration of justice than the regular courts. As there is no delay in the disposal of cases, these systems of justice are more effective. In tribal councils the cases are decided on the spot, and on the day of meeting usually no case continues for more than a week or so. After the interaction of the two tribal groups it is felt that there are only a few cases which result in miscarriage of justice. Though quick, the tribals are properly conducted in the presence of villagers at open meetings. Everyone is free to state facts and any lie or misstatement is likely to be contradicted right on the spot.

Another important feature of tribal justice is its cheapness in expenditure, compared to the expensive system of trial at regular courts. It is cheap, because of its inherent, simple procedure. As trials are mostly held in the area where both the parties and witnesses reside, people are not obliged to keep away from their vocations of life for a long period. So on that account they are not made to suffer loss in many respects. In trials no cost is involved in bringing witnesses before the tribal council.

The cost of the litigation is almost nil. The trial before the concerned tribal council is simple and not procedure-bound. It is in accordance with the customary laws which the tribes understand. The village council can give an ex-party decision if the other party is willfully absent.

The tribal councils ensure maintenance of social order among themselves. The village officials of the council, non-tribal organisations. Panchayat officials and police officials categorically assert that the systems of justice are good and that the tribals would not like to give up the systems. These have stood the test of time. They meet the present-day needs to a great extent. The systems are by and large effective. The effectiveness in due not only to people's faith in, and satisfaction with these systems, but also due to their active participation in them. There is nothing wrong with the systems of public trials by untrained persons of sound commonsense.

It is indeed surprising to see how these rather primitive people have developed this modern concept of restitution through the workings of their simple, prompt and inexpensive system of justice, which seeks to rehabilitate the victim through compensation for the injury done to him. We have to admit that the tribal groups have faith in the system as well as in the social customs and religious rites which they unhesitatively accept.

Chapter Five

CONCLUSION

I

Hunger, anger, fear and *libido,* i.e., sex drive are considered to be the basic instincts of the animals of which man is one. As time rolled on, adaptation to different situations crystallised and we find different cultural scenarios. Among the Eskimo, killing the old invalid ancestor is not a crime, rather it indicates that killing and consuming the flesh of the seniormost member of the community will give the younger generation more energy and experience. Among the Kutia Konds of Orissa human sacrifice was a custom - it was known as *Meriah* - the human being would be sacrificed for better rainfall and greater prosperity of the county. *Meriahs* are regarded as sacred beings.

> Consecration of *Meriah* took place about a fortnight before the sacrifice - his hair was cut for the first time and he was crowned with flowers. During the week before the sacrifice, the crowd had complete licence to indulge in unlimited debauchery... On fatal day preceding the sacrifice, the *Meriah* was led to a grove, outside the village. Here, he is tied with his face towards a forked pillar. His head was pulled down between the prongs of the fork and he was anointed with oil. His body was smeared with turmeric paste. Every

> celebrant at the festival now eagerly touched the consecreated body of the Meriah for good luck.
>
> - (Watts : 1970 : The Halfclad tribals of Eastern India)

And thus human sacrifice is made for prosperity and goodluck of the people. Naturally, crime, murder, sacrifice, etc. are considered to be relative terms. Examples from the Naga headhunters or the Mariah Gonds of Baster are not rare. So the nature of crime differs from society to society alongwith the nature of punishment. After twelve years, if draught spoils the crop, then human sacrifice was made among the Oraons-an Dravidian speaking tribe of Chotanagpur.

Malinowski (London : 1970) states :

> If the rules of custom are obeyed by the savage through sheer inability to break them, no definition can be given of law, no distinction can be drawn between rules of law, morals, manners and other usages. For the only way in which we can classify rules of conduct is by reference to the motives and sanctions by which they are enforced. So that with the assumption of an automatic obedience to all custom, anthropology has to give up any attempt at introducing into the facts, order and classification, which is the first task of science.
>
> (*Crime and Custom in Savage Society*, p. 50)

Sidney Hartland (1921) expresses the view that many more actions of the tribals can be viewed as 'primitive prelogical mentality—due to shapelessness of early culture'. It is accepted that savages have a class of obligatory rules, not endowed with any mystical character, not set forth in:

> "the name of God, not enforced by any supernatural saction, but provided with a purely social binding force."
>
> (p. 51 : Malinowski : 1940)

It is said that the people, i.e., the tribal communities feel a strong respect for all of them, has (sic) a tendency to do what others do, what everyone approves or and not drawn or driven in another direction by his appetites or interests will follow the biddings of custom rather than any other course. (*Ibid,* 52)

For the code of Moses, familiarity called the Mosaic code, prescribes a stern way of punishment to the wrongdoer by way of retaliation. "An eye for an eye : a tooth for a tooth."

> "Murder can be avenged by next-of kin according to the notions of the day by the relations of the deceased person as a matter of duty and necessarily by the state and the avenger was deemed to be guiltless. An outraged husband who catches red handed his wife and her paramour in the very act of adultery was considered to be fully justified in killing them both, then and there. As times progressed the conception of blood-fued was abolished. Throughout Hittite code the principle was restitution and not retribution."
>
> (Raghaviah : *Tribal Justice* 1968, Hyderabad)

We also accept the terms, sin, crime and tort. Sin is offence against supernatural power. Offence against the community is crime and offence against the individual is tort. Of course, rules and regulations have been laid down for governing the affairs of families in several matters like marriage, adoption, inheritance, which often give rise to family disputes.

Herakiri was in vogue in Japan when the emperor was to present the culprit with a daggar, ceremoniously, for committing suicide. In the Babylonian code body mutation was common. Even in India in the Mauryan days, hands were cut off for theft. Similarly, severe sentences were passed for other crimes also.

II

It has been advocated by Verrier Elwin in his *A Philosophy for NEFA* (1960) that an important means of delivering the tribal people from a sense of inferiority is to strengthen their own system of government and to recognise and establish their own forms of jurisprudence and administration of justice. In this connection it can be said that ideas of guilt and crime vary from tribe to tribe. It is also reported that the fines which the individual is unable to pay are shared by the entire group of clansmen.

It is a recorded fact that the main cause of the Santal rebellion of 1885 was the unsatisfactory dispensation of justice by the British in India. There are indeed many evidences of tribal unrest in India, caused by the deprivation of legitimate dues suffered by the tribals.

In NEFA area, the regulation of 1995 vests in the Political Officer, the Assistant Political Officer and the village authorities the power of the administration of criminal justice. There the councils are empowered to try cases of theft and simple injury-the councils have civil powers and can try all civil suits.

However, customary laws always prevail before the councils. Crimes like murder, kidnapping and rape should therefore be dealt with by payment of compensation in accordance with the tribal customary laws. In this connection it can be remembered that the 1945 regulation has toned down the severity of the punishments inflicted by tribal courts. Punishment for the murder of Tamali Soren (Santal girl) in West Bengal is a case in point.

III

Study of the laws and legal customs of the tribals is rather neglected in Anthropological investigations, though a recent publication entitled *Tribal Ethnography: Customary Law and Change* (Delhi-1993) under the guidance of K.S. Singh is an important book in this regard. The Law Research Institute of Gauhati under the guidance of Prof. M.C. Goswami is also worth mentioning in this context.

The constitution of India alongwith the Scheduled tribes was given importance in the report of the Dhebar commission (1960-61). The report is being considered by the administration to overcome many difficulties. After independence people have become conscious and the tribals are getting more advantages when the Ministry of Welfare (T.D.) take a special interest in involving the scholars to undertake investigations of unstudied areas related to tribal life. It has been accepted that the problems of the tribals all over the country are not the same. These differ from place to place. Study of the people on the hills or in isolated places or in the plain areas differs, because these people are in interaction with different groups of people at different degrees. It has been reiterated that many more tribals became converted, or shifted to urban settings and we get plenty of examples of inter-community marriages. Besides, urbanisation, changes of residence for higher education and service have become important and thus we can expect many additional changes in the traditional life of the people.

As we have assumed, the customary tribal laws once known and codified will throw light on the inter-relationship pattern existing among the members of the tribal communities. At the same time land and property laws will be framed and this will help to reduce the number of litigations and other difficulties of the tribals. Accurate compilation of customs and traditions, having the 'force of law', is undoubtedly a serious proposition.

Penetration into the heart of the customs or traditions is extremely important, though careful ethnographers try their best to interpret the customs and discuss them properly.

IV

It has been observed that through various ethnographic accounts we have been acquainted with many more customs prevalent among the tribals. At the same time we have an idea about the changes due to spread of education and new employment opportunities. All these together have brought about some definite development in the tribal life in general. Santal customary laws have been studied in detail along with various ethnographic accounts which reflect various aspects of tribal life just to project a lucid picture of the system. It is to be noted that an interpretation of the system and the nature of accommodation of the groups into the system should be given greater priority. It is true that the major areas of the customary laws are marriage, divorce, property, succession and adoption, maintenance and guardianship. We have seen the importance of the indigenous justice system and the effectiveness of customary laws among the tribal groups, the nature of redressal of grievances, the convenience of resorting to the panchayats, police and the courts, judicial responses and impact of non-tribal law on the customary laws of the people under survey. More emphasis has been placed on the West Bengal situation where democratic panchayats are functioning for more than 20 years. The tribals are happy with the present system where non-tribals often take part in many decision-making areas. The tribals' view in respect of ethnicity has been minimised in the process of gradual accommodation into the broader social system.

It is to be understood that the panchayats, police, and the courts vary from place to place. Much depends upon the location of the villages, educational standard of the villagers, their political consciousness and influence of the non-tribal neighbours upon the tribal groups. Many of the tribals can afford to go to the court and we have seen how they make use of the court to vindicate their rights. It has been noted also that sometimes they come to the court straight without referring the problematic matter to the village council. This shows that community pressure is decreasing and the confidence in the indigenous justice system has been shaken in some peripheral villages.

V

In the belief system of the tribals, we find the roles of the evil eye, evil mouth and the witch craft. We get many examples of witch craft in the districts specially West Midnapur, Bankura and Purulia. It is true that witch craft has an important place in the life of the Santals, whereas in other tribal communities this belief exists—but not in such a degree as among the Santals. Mahalis, Koras, Lodhas or others believe in witchcraft, *dain,* sorcerer and their role in the life of the people. Many more fabulous stories are there and these are handed down through generations. The Santals surrender to the village *Janguru* who suggests the causes. Lodhas and Bhumij believe in witchcraft but not with the same intensity or gravity as the Santals or Mahalis. All of them believe in *Ojhas* (Sorcerer) - those who can foresee the causes of the diseases or difficulties. The *Gunins* in Munda and Lodha societies are very common; they consult the village priests or other persons who can diagnose and suggest remedial measures. Thus customs in relation to these beliefs are still in vogue, though local medical help is also available.

Another important factor is the economy of the people. Many of them say that they have no capacity to go to the good allopathic physician, hence they have to depend on *Gunins* or Sorcerers or *Ojhas*. Even on festive occasions some people become spirit-possessed. At the time, their bodies become stiff and spasms appear, they constantly shake heads and have foaming mouths. They answer many more bewildering questions or suggest remedial measures as to how the serious problems can be overcome. Their reply is considered to be the reply of the spirits. The replies are - considered as authentic as in the case of the *Jangurus* of the Santals. This belief system interwined the customs, traditions and the people. Thus we have to admit that these beliefs bound the people to a system and the people have no alternative but to accept them. As a result, the witches are killed mercilessly as per the Santal belief.

For having the required training of the witches, the Santal girls are taken by force and are initiated into witchcraft. They are taken to the *Bonga* and taught songs and *mantras*. As per the Santal proverb the *Bonga* (spirit) marries the witches. The chief witch does harm to the girls who do not intend to become witches. She teaches the black art of killing men and animals and destroying others' property. They cook-rice together with fowls and afterwards offer the same to the *Bonga*. They eat together. At dead of night they meet. Unless the black magic is completely learnt, they continue to meet for rehearsal daily in the forest or near a sacred grove. It is believed that if a girl comes out with a witch and there upon decides not be a witch, other witches will kill her. However, the witch is popularly known as *'dan'*. In this way there are systematic training procedure to become a witch. Gradually, her harmful tendencies become known to all. This art of becoming a witch is a custom in the tribal society. Among the Lodhas the belief in witches is strong. The witches are also known as *daini*. They are believed to have ever-changing shapes; sometimes they take the form of a dog or of a cat. The spirit in the shape of a cat enters a house. If by chance it casts a look upon a child, the poor victim begins to wither from that day and at last dies. Of course, if it is detected early, then treatment is not impossible. At dead of night, specially in the darker part of night, the witches are believed to walk naked on two hands, putting the legs upwards, and consume fresh human excreta. If any person finds her and removes her clothes and puts fire on these the witch will surely die.

Other tribals like, the Munda, Mahali and Kora also believe in witches and there are always some systematic formalities to overcome the problems pertaining to them. It is to be remembered that the belief system as well as the method of training continues in tribal societies.

VI

In respect of comparison or provision of the customary laws with the laws of the present Indian penal code, one can say that the Indian penal code runs parallel to the Santal customary law in some cases, but in some other cases both are in conflict, with each other. Marriage by elopement. (Santal - *Apangir*) is still in practice under the Santal customary law, but it is in sharp conflict with Section 366 of the Indian penal code. When a boy elopes with a girl under eighteen, he commits an offence under this section. These days boys are sometimes looked under Section 366 I.P.C. The Santal men are also charged for enticing or taking away a married woman under Section 498 I.P.C. Under the Santal customary law such offences are punishable with fine. Again, when a Santal boy marries a girl under sixteen by capturing her he becomes guilty of the offence of kidnapping under

Section 363 of the Indian penal code. Moreover, keeping an abducted girl by the parents amounts to an offence under Section 368 I.P.C.

Records of the court reveal that when the bride has deserted the husband but the bride-price or the brother's due or customary gifts have not been returned to the husband's father, the bridegroom's party goes to bride's village and forcibly takes away cattle from there. It is prescribed under the Santal customary laws. In such cases some Santals had to face trial and suffer imprisonment for offences under Section 379/380 of Indian penal code, 1860. This is because the bride's party reported the matter to the police. Outraging the modesty of a Santal girl during a festival or dance is not a grave offence under Santal customary laws, but Section 354 I.P.C. has provision for punishment for such offences. Such cases were previously dealt with by the village council.

However, there are a few such cases among the Santals, whereas all these are not present among the other tribals. We have to accept that since custom contemplates legal relationships it must be subjected to review by the constituted judicial authorities which control all legal relationships. Hence the courts' function is to supervise the custom, in the ordinary terminology of jurisprudence. Interpreters of customs are generally described as jurists. Jurists are not only the writers on legal topics but also those whose special function is to expound and apply customary law. (Allen C.K. 1964: Law in the making, Oxford).

The relation between an indigenous customary law and technical treatment of it is one of action and reaction. The materials with which the judge as an interpreter has to deal are not manufactured by him, they grow spontaneously out of a fundamental legal relationship and out of certain characteristic habits of mind in the community oriented towards law. In modern society courts scrutinise the custom as an existing rule of conduct. If satisfied by its scrutiny, the court recognises the custom as being valid (Allen, 1964 : Law in the making, Oxford). It is to be noted that the courts abrogate customs which are analysis of the leading case-laws would reveal run counter to the nature of tribal customary laws. Law has to adopt itself to the habits and customs of the people. Marriage by exchange has been recognised by the court as legal and valid. Time and again, aboriginal customs have been scrutinised by the court.

It is to be noted that the Santals or many other tribes do not view the court favourably. It has been seen in our field work that they attest to their perception. They say, that the court is very slow. It is a place where we are exploited by the lawyers and touts. A few tribals mention that they have been falsely implicated by the rival party and some say that when the village council cannot do justice they resort to the court of law, but inordinate delay frustrates them to a great extent.

VII

Customs reflect norms and values of the society. Customs may be good or evil, or both. Societies, whether developed or primitive, are replete with customs. There is no codification of customs in primitive societies except a few, as cited early. However, customs may be classified in different groups, namely legal and conventional, general and local class customs and family customs. Study of customary laws is very important not only among the tribes but among other groups, especially the Hindu castes and Muslims. It is acknowledged that custom is a source and form of law. It is very difficult to trace the origin of a custom which is lost in mystery. Custom is the oldest form of law-making, showing the continuing course of conduct observed by the community. Anthropologically custom is a totality of socially-acquired behaviour patterns.

There are many juristic theories on customary law. The historical school holds that customary law is a spontaneous expression of the genius of people. Customary law is followed because it is convenient, conducive and helpful to society. It is believed that the so-called primitive people feared to do anything that might violate these rules. This would offend the gods. Of course, it is accepted by the anthropologists that custom and law are inter-twined with each other. There is a thin line of difference between the two. Both custom and law guide relationships. Sanction of law comes from the state, which may involve physical coercion. Custom is sanctioned by a particular society. It is the traditional and indigenous system of social control. It originates from the repetitive performance of a particular behaviour or habit. Philosophers look at it as a subject of normative ethics. There are different views regarding the relationship of law and custom. Some scholars say that law and custom contradict other. It is admitted that custom is the oldest institution of the world. In each and every society of the world, the role of custom is recognised and valued.

Hindu law custom has been regarded as the most important source of law. Hindu kings were advised to respect immemorial customs of every province and to overrule them if they were contrary to the sacred law. Hindu law of succession and inheritance which ultimately got codified in the Hindu succession act of 1956 was based on the customary laws of *Dayabhaga* and *Mitakshara* Schools. Section 2 (2) of the Hindu succession act and Hindu marriage act recognise customary laws practised by the tribes. Hindu marriage act has also been codified. Customary laws relating to marriage and divorce have been recognised by the act.

The constitution of India provides for preservation and maintenance of customary laws in Articles 244, 244A, 371A and fifth and sixth schedules. Moreover, there are many central and state acts, which protect and preserve tribal customary laws. Section-I, sub-section-3 of the code of civil procedure 1908 and Section-I, sub-section-3 of the code of criminal procedure, 1973 also provide for application of customary laws in the tribal area.

Time and again, the validity of custom has been challenged in the courts of the law and the courts have held that the following are essentials of custom : antiquity, continuity, certainity, reasonability, morality. Moreover, the courts have added two more essential features: Custom must not be opposed to public policy and to law. A person who pleads for the existence of a custom has to prove it as there is no presumption in favour of custom. Section-13, 32(4), 48, 49 of Indian evidence act. provides for rules regarding the proof of custom. Custom is a question of fact. When there is a question whether the custom is prevailing in any particular tribe or not it can best be answered by the tribesmen themselves. Theories of custom do not help the courts much in deciding the existence of a custom.

It is a fact that customary law is more pronounced in a tribal society than in an advanced society. Marriage, succession, inheritance, adoption, guardianship and maintenance are guided by customary laws in tribal society. Custom is the life-blood of the tribesmen. It regulates social relationships. It is a means of social control.

VIII

It has been stated that the tribal communities have their democratic indigenous justice systems to serve their social purpose. These non-formal institutions are embedded in their customary law. The village councils settle the disputes among the villagers and interpret and apply their customary laws. The councils are unique and unparalleled in dispensing simple, cheap, expeditious remedies to the villagers. They have survived for generations with their useful attributes. Having regard to their requirements of a simple tribal society and its conventional crimes like trespass, mischief, assault, theft and customary offences, the systems are well serving the tribal communities and are still useful to them.

Of course, each system has its merits and demerits. Hence, tribal justice has also its limitations and shortcomings. But the justice systems are suited to society for maintenance of order. They also ensure peace and tranquility.

By way of conclusion it can be said that customary law regulates social relations amongst the members of the society. It facilitates social control. A breach of customary law forms the subject matter of dispute and may lead to serious consequences. It is appreciated that the justice systems are cheap and uncomplicated and assure expeditions remedies to the villagers.

It is important to note that due to the panchayati raj in West Bengal, many more non-tribals are gradually penetrating. As a result, the strong tribalism is in a state of erosion. Customary law does not determine the majority by age. It is generally accepted among the tribals that if a boy is capable of earning his own livelihood by his manual labour he is regarded as an adult. A married girl living with her husband is treated as an adult. Of course, there are evidences against killing of the witches when tribals achieve education. He is found to fight against the dangerous idea of witchcraft. The panchayats and police sometimes save the alleged witches and sometimes the police files chargesheet against the assailants in the court of law. Of course, the grounds for alleging and suspecting witchcraft are superstition, personal grudge, hatred, jealousy, greed, land hunger, political fued, exploitation, etc.

Impact of Hindu law and culture is quite clear on the customary laws of these tribal groups. Their customary laws are still uncodified although. They are being practised since olden days. There are variation of customary laws as prevalent in Santal parganas or the bordering districts.

Of course, it is seen that the customary laws are in a process of change. Social and economic factors along with some strong political factors are responsible for this change. It is noticed that most of these changes are due to local needs and nature of political pressures.

The spread of education, new employment facilities and staying either in urban areas or in different places are also considered as reasons for changes in the customary laws. *Bitlaha* is in vogue among the Santals to take mass revenge, as it took place sometime ago at Nayagram police station of Midnapur, West Bengal when about 17 Lodhas were killed at broad daylight. Even the Police Officers could not restrain the furious mob as they declared their retributive scheme early by sending branches of *Sal* trees. In actual time, all the tribals and even some non-tribals assembled and attacked the Lodhas who were suspected not only of stealing but of outraging the modesty of Santal women. Of course, the police could not stop the mass killing; afterwards only rehabilitation measures were taken.

Anyway, we have considered the new circumstances in West Bengal when education has spread, communication facilities have developed and last of all, new panchayati, i.e., democracy has been working for 20 years under the leadership of the left-front ministry.

By way of conclusion it can be said that in spite of all these advantages, customary laws among the tribals have still to play an important role as these are difficult to separate from the life and culture of the tribals. Of course, there should be encouragement on the part of the government to study witchcraft *dain,* sorcerer among these groups of people and to find out measures to do away with the associated problems. The school teachers should be there to overcome the problems related to their social life. Another suggestion is that in the schools, where most of the tribal children read (both primary and secondary), arrangements should be made to provide at least one tribal teacher. This will help the students to think that their own man is there and through this teacher many prejudices may be removed. Though the Linguistic commission is there still, Ministry of Welfare (T.D.) should take more interest in tuning the minds of the young folk. They must not be conservative; they must have a scientific bent of mind. Nothing new can be imposed upon their customary laws but they can be redesigned slowly be developing a scientific outlook for the benefit of the society in which the tribal communities live.

REFERENCES

1. Archer, W.B., 1984 — *Tribal Law and Justice: A report on the Santal,* Delhi.
2. Atchuthen, P.S., 1985 — *Jurisprudence and Legal Theory,* Lucknow.
3. Bajpaee, S.C., 1987 — *Lahaul : Spiti : a Forbidden land in the Himalayas,* New Delhi.
4. Bhatia, S.C. (ed.), 1991 — *Law and Social Action,* Delhi University.
5. Bhowmick, P.K., 1992 — *The Chenchus,* Calcutta.
6. Bodding, P.O., 1916 — *How the Santals Live,* Royal Asiatic Society of Bengal, Calcutta.
7. Bodding, P.O., 1929 — *How the Santals Live,* Royal Asiatic Society of Bengal, Calcutta.
8. Bodding, P.O., 1935 — *Traditions and Institutions of the Santals,* Oslo Ethnographic Museum.
9. Bordoloi, B.N., 1984 — *The Dimasa Kacharis of Assam,* Gauhati Tribal Research Institute, Assam.
10. Bose, J.K., 1980 — *Glimpses of Tribal Life in N.E. India,* Calcutta.

11. Brown, R., 1922 — *The Andaman Islanders*, London.

12. Campbell, A., 1905 — *Rules of Succession and Partition of Property as observed by Santals*. J. Bihar and Orissa Research Institute.

13. Choudhuri, A.B., 1985 — *Santal Samaj Daini O Bartaman Sankat* in Bengali, Calcutta.

14. Census of India, 1991 — New Delhi.

15. Chattopadhyay, S.K., 1928 — *Languages and Linguistic Problem*. Oxford University Press.

16. Dalton, E.I. Reprint, 1972 — *Descriptive Ethnology of Bengal*, Calcutta.

17. Das, T.C., 1953 — Social Organisation of the Tribal Peoples in the *Indian Journal of Social Work*, Bombay.

18. Edward, S., 1954 — 'Custom' in Edwin R.A. Seligman and Alvin in *Encyclopaedia* in Social Sciences, Vol. III, Macmillan, N.Y.

19. Encyclopaedia of the Social Sciences, 1959 — Macmillan and Company, New York.

20. Goswami, M.C., 1979 — *The Customary Law and Practices of the AO of Nagaland*. Gauhati Law Research Institute.

21. Haimendorf, C.V., 1976 — *Return to the Naked Nagas*. New Delhi.

22. Hazra, D., 1983 — *The Kolam of Yeotmal,* Calcutta.

23. Hutton, J.H., 1935 — *The Sema Nagas.* Oxford University Press, London.

24. Kusum, K. and Bakshi, P.M., 1982 — *Customary Law and Justice in Tribal Areas of Meghalaya,* Bombay.

25. Macphail, R.C. (ed), 1988 — *Santali English Dictionary,* Calcutta.

26. Maine, H.S., 1921 Reprint : 1985 — *Early Law and Customs,* Delhi.

27. Maine, H.S., 1988 — *Ancient Law.* Oxford University Press, London.

28. Malinowski, B., 1940 — *Sex and Repression in Savage Society,* London.

29. Malinowski, B., 1949 — *Sex and Repression in Savage Society,* London.

30. Radcliffe-Brown, A.R., 1964 — *Structure and Function in Primitive Society,* London.

31. Raghavia, V., 1968 — *Tribal Justice* T.C.R. and Training Institute Hyderabad.

32. Risley, H.H., 1981 — *Tribes and Castes of Bengal,* Vol. II, Caicutta.

33. Rivers, W.H.R., 1932 — *Social Organisation,* London.

34. Sahu, L.N., 1949 — *Fifth Schedule of the Draft Constitution.* Govt. of India.

35. Sengupta, S.K., 1960 *The Social Profiles of the Mahalis*, Calcutta.

36. Singh, K.S. (ed.), 1993 *Tribal Ethnography Customary Law and Change*, New Delhi.

Index